THE STATE

THE STATE

FRANZ OPPENHEIMER

Translated by John Gitterman
Introduction by Charles Hamilton
Introduction to this Edition by George H. Smith

A FREE LIFE EDITIONS BOOK

Fox &
Wilkes
San Francisco

This "Authorized Translation" of *The State* was first
published by The Bobbs-Merrill Company in 1914.

Introduction to the Free Life Edition © 1975 by
Charles H. Hamilton.

This edition © 1997 by Fox & Wilkes
938 Howard Street, Ste. 202
San Francisco, CA 94103.

All Rights Reserved.

ISBN 0-930073-22-3 (hc)
ISBN 0-930073-23-1 (pb)

Printed in the United States of America.

Contents

INTRODUCTION TO THIS EDITION

Mention the word "anarchy" in polite society and most people will think of chaos. Explain that by "anarchy" you mean a "society without government," and you will be met with blank stares. "Yes," you will be reminded, "that's what we said—chaos."

This identification of anarchy with chaos is deeply imbedded in the popular mind and rarely results from conscious deliberation. It is tacit rather than explicit, part of that amorphous but formidable jumble of folklore, prejudice and dogma that goes by various names: "public opinion," "current opinion," "spirit of the age," "collective consciousness," "common sense," and more.

Anarchy means chaos—this popular myth is self-evident to the popular mind. From this tacit axiom there flows another: government is indispensable to social order, the only thing that stands between civilization and barbarism. Some kind of government, no matter how corrupt or despotic, is always better than no government at all. Indeed, the most serious charge that can be made against a government is that it has degenerated into "anarchy." Fuzzy thinking always benefits the status quo. Man is born into a world of social institutions which he tends to accept as natural and inevitable. Few people are motivated to question the legitimacy of established institutions.

A major task of political philosophy has been to justify the State. Such an enterprise, whatever the outcome, strikes most people as absurd, because its strips the State of its axiomatic status. To ask whether the State should exist reflects a curiosity and skepticism that are foreign to the popular mind. The State simply does exist, like rocks and trees and birds. We might as well ask whether civilization should exist. David Hume put it well:

> Any one, who finding the impossibility of accounting for the right of the
> present [government], by any receiv'd system of ethics, shou'd resolve to
> deny absolutely that right, and assert, that it is not authoriz'd by morality,

wou'd be justly thought to maintain a very extravagant paradox, and to shock the common sense and judgment of mankind. (*Treatise*, 558)

The preceding factors contribute to what I call the tacit legitimation of the State. As an established institution the State enjoys a presumption of legitimacy. Anyone who questions the State on a fundamental level must defeat this presumption. The critic has the burden of proof; he must prove his case beyond a reasonable doubt or be overwhelmed by the current of public opinion and tacit legitimation.

The libertarian critic faces another obstacle. Much of the case for individual liberty is highly abstract—indeed, liberty itself is not a concept that is easily mastered. Some of the essential components of libertarian theory, such as spontaneous order, seem to defy common sense. Philosophic and economic reasoning is not easily digested, nor can it always be chopped into slogans and soundbites.

People are disinclined to labor needlessly, and reasoning is mental labor. Most people will believe cultural folklore rather than strain their brains with original thoughts. As Bertrand Russell once said, most people would rather die than think; in fact, many do.

Not everything is bleak for the libertarian. He is heir to a remarkable system of ideas—a constellation of theories in ethics, politics, economics, sociology, and other disciplines. Intellectuals, as Adam Smith pointed out, are often drawn to a system of ideas because of its aesthetic qualities, and in this regard the theory of liberty has little competition. And as Alexis de Tocqueville says:

> What has made so many men, since untold ages, stake their all on liberty is its intrinsic glamour, a fascination it has in itself, apart from all "practical" considerations. . . . The man who asks of freedom anything other than itself is born to be a slave. (168–69)

Libertarians have long felt the need to educate themselves in various disciplines, and many have become proficient writers. Despite the best of plans, however, the spread of an ideology is highly susceptible to the slings and arrows of unintended consequences.

Franz Oppenheimer's *The State* is an excellent illustration of un-planned benefits. Though by no means a best-seller, this fairly difficult work has influenced a variety of radical intellectuals. Oppenheimer's influence is measured not by the number of his readers but by their quality. Albert Jay Nock drew liberally from Oppenheimer in his great work, *Our Enemy, the State*. Other influential libertarians, such as Walter Grinder and Murray Rothbard, have stressed the importance of Oppenheimer as well, and thereby extended his influence to a much wider audience.

The ideas of Oppenheimer were disseminated by fellow intellectuals, who in turn influenced thousands of their readers. This ideological ripple effect was unforeseeable, but it happened because Oppenheimer wrote like the scholar he was, rather than writing simplistic pap in the hope of reaching a popular audience.

Franz Oppenheimer investigated the origin of primitive states, but he failed to discuss the relevance of his investigation. Even if we assume that all States originated in conquest, does this have any implications for political theory? Anarchists in particular have used the conquest theory as a rationale to condemn the State, but, as we shall see, the conquest theory, or any theory about the origin of the State, does not necessarily lead to particular conclusions about the desirability or legitimacy of the State. To move from a theory of the *origin* of the State to a theory of the *justification* of the State would be to commit the "genetic fallacy." How an idea or institution originated is an issue distinct from the present justification of that idea or institution.

This does not mean that historical analysis is irrelevant to a theory of the State. On the contrary, only through historical investigation can we understand the nature of an institution. This is where the analogy between a belief and an institution, as illustrated in the genetic fallacy, breaks down. A belief exists in the mind of the believer, and this belief, whatever its origin or history, can reasonably be examined for coherence, evidence, logic, etc. The same is not true of institutions. We cannot even know what an institution is without some knowledge of its history. Institutions are defined with reference to habitualized patterns of action, and such patterns always imply a past. Social institutions, as such, exist only in the minds of those who perceive them; and we cannot begin to understand why large groups of people share similar mental constructs unless we understand the historical problems and processes that generated a common system of ideas. If sufficiently large numbers of people stopped perceiving the State, that institution would cease to exist. True, persons would still exist who claim to act on behalf of the State, but their coercive actions would no longer enjoy legitimacy in the public eye. Those agents would be indistinguishable from bands of robbers and other outlaws. The coercive actions of the State are distinguished by their legitimacy, and such legitimacy can result from nothing more than the beliefs of individuals. A State without legitimacy could not "tax," it could only steal; it could not wage "war," it could only murder; it could not "conscript," it could only enslave. Like Santa Claus, the State can exist only as long as people believe in it.

Viewed from this perspective, to investigate the origin of the State is to investigate the origin of a belief system.

OPPENHEIMER'S ACCOUNT

States have varied considerably in their structure and jurisdiction, but all of them fit the description given by Franz Oppenheimer. The State originates in conquest—in the subjugation of peasant farmers by nomadic herdsman. "[T]he cause of the genesis of all States is the contrast between peasants and herdsman, between laborers and robbers, between bottom lands and prairies." (26)[1]

The State originates in conquest, and maintains itself through exploitation. Oppenheimer distinguishes two basic methods of acquiring wealth: the economic means (labor and voluntary exchange) and the political means ("the unrequited appropriation of the labor of others"). This leads to a succinct description: "The state is an organization of the political means." (15) The State, for Oppenheimer, is organized theft; a method of systematic plunder. This is true but incomplete. The State is a union of thieves, but not all such unions are States. State theft is distinguished by being legitimized; i.e., its coercive actions are generally regarded by the subject population as morally and/or legally proper. This feature is emphasized by Max Weber in his classic discussion of the modern State:

> A "ruling organization" will be called "political" insofar as its existence and order is continuously safeguarded within a given *territorial* area by the threat and application of physical force on the part of the administrative state. A compulsory political organization with continuous operations . . . will be called a "state" insofar as its administrative staff successfully upholds the claim to the *monopoly* of the *legitimate* use of physical force in the enforcement of its order. (54)

CONQUEST THEORIES OF THE ORIGIN OF THE STATE

Conquest theories of the origination of the state are nothing new. Some early Christian apologists traced the origin of the Roman Empire to war and conquest, and during the eleventh century, as pope and emperor waged a war of words in the "Investiture Controversy," Pope Gregory VII emphasized the violent origin of earthly kingdoms. Some versions of conquest theory also appeared after the mid-thirteenth century, when the history of governments became a popular subject. According to Tholommeo of Lucca, all governments originated in conquest, but they acquired legitimacy as they became useful.

The conquest theory of State formation entered modern political philosophy in the sixteenth century statement of this thesis in Jean Bodin's *Six Books of the Commonwealth*:

> Reason and common sense alike point to the conclusion that the origin and foundation of commonwealths was in force and violence. If this is not enough, it can be shown on the testimony of historians . . . that the first generations of men were unacquainted with the sentiments of honor, and their highest endeavor was to kill, torture, rob, and enslave their fellows. (19)

Less well known than Bodin's account is that of Blaise Pascal. Man's corrupt nature, thoroughly vitiated by original sin, harbors a desire to rule over others, Pascal argued, but only a few are able to accomplish this. "Might is the sovereign of the world," declared Pascal, and he continued with a clear statement of the conquest theory:

> Let us, then, imagine we see society in the process of formation. Men will doubtless fight till the stronger party overcomes the weaker, and a dominant party is established. But when this is once determined, the masters, who do not desire the continuation of strife, then decree that the power which is in their hands shall be transmitted as they please. Some place it in election by the people, others in hereditary succession, etc. (87)

Man's corrupted reason can no longer discern the true law of justice, according to Pascal, so mankind is ruled by custom, not reason. Social order requires blind obedience to established laws, solely because they have the force of habitual custom and are routinely accepted by the masses. Custom, declared Pascal forthrightly, "creates the whole of equity, for the simple reason that it is accepted." The justification of law is self-contained: "it is the law and nothing more."

Pascal thought it hazardous to examine the foundation of law too closely, because those in quest of a justice that is natural and universal will invariably be disappointed as they discover the relativity, inconstancy, and hypocrisy of man-made laws and customs. For example:

> Why do you kill me? What! do you not live on the other side of the water? If you lived on this side, my friend, I should be an assassin, and it would be unjust to slay you in this manner. But since you live on the other side, I am a hero, and it is just. (83)

Earthly rulers acquired power through violence and bloodshed, Pascal argued, but people "must not see the fact of usurpation" or they will "shake off the yoke as soon as they recognize it." Law should be obeyed not because it is just but because it is useful to maintain social order: "law was once introduced without reason, and has become reasonable."

As Pascal explained, custom is the foundation of governmental legitimacy:

> The habit of seeing kings accompanied by guards, drums, officers, and all the paraphernalia which mechanically inspire respect and awe, makes their countenance, when sometimes seen alone without these accompaniments, impress respect and awe on their subjects; because we cannot separate in thought their persons from the surroundings with which we see them usually joined. And the world, which knows not that the effect is the result of habit, believes that it arises by a natural force. (87)

Pascal's discussion is virtually forgotten, yet it is remarkably similar to David Hume's views on custom, the violent origins of government, and utility as the foundation of law. Although Hume's celebrated essays are usually cited as the source of his conquest theory, we find the same interpretation in his youthful (and greatest) work, *A Treatise of Human Nature*:

> 'Tis certain, that if we remount to the first origin of every nation, we shall find, that there scarce is any race of kings, or form of a commonwealth, that is not primarily founded on usurpation and rebellion, and whose title is not at first worse than doubtful and uncertain. Time alone gives solidity to their right; and operating gradually on the minds of men, reconciles them to any authority, and makes it seem just and reasonable. (556)

In 1750 Anne-Robert-Jacques Turgot delivered a discourse titled *On Universal History* for the theological faculty at the University of Paris. This pathbreaking work explained social progress as an unintended byproduct of conflict and narrow self-interest. According to Turgot, men's "passions, even their fits of rage, have led them on their way without their being aware of where they were going."

> The first [governments] were necessarily the product of war, and thus implied government by one man alone. We need not believe that men ever voluntarily gave themselves *one master*. (69)

Another Frenchman, the historian Augustin Thierry (1795–1856), asserted that every nation has been "created by the mixture of several races: the race of the invaders . . . and the race of those invaded." This view led Thierry and other French liberals, notably Charles Comte and Charles Dunoyer, to develop a theory of class analysis involving two political groups: the rulers and the ruled. Ironically perhaps, these French Liberals influenced the thinking of Karl Marx.[2]

The conquest theory was forcefully defended by Johann Herder, for whom the State originated in war and "conquest by violence," and by Friedrich Nietzsche, who believed that the "State originates in the cruelest way through conquest."

One form of the "external conflict" theory is that advanced by Herbert Spencer, among others, which attributes the formation of the primitive state to the temporary submission to a leader in time of war. Through time these warlords became permanent chieftains and kings, as they legitimated their power by appealing to supernatural powers.

The German sociologist Ludwig Gumplowicz, whom Oppenheimer called the "pathfinder" of modern conquest theory (11), developed the conquest theory in great detail; indeed, he called it the "corner stone" of sociological theory. "[E]very political organization . . . begins at the moment when one horde permanently subjugates another." (125–6)

The State, according to Gumplowicz, begins with the forced subjection of one group by another: "The state . . . is the subjection of one social group by another and the establishment of sovereignty." (199)

Primitive peoples, according to Gumplowicz, lived in small kinship groups and followed traditional customary law. Modern law, in contrast, was imposed by the victorious group on their victims; it was institutionalized repression whereby the victorious group could efficiently exploit their victims. There was no room here for a doctrine of natural rights; indeed, natural rights were "overthrown, dead, buried." Similarly, "equality is incompatible with the State and is a complete negation of it." (263)

OPPENHEIMER'S CRITICS

The reception given to Oppenheimer's statement of the conquest theory was very mixed. Alexander Rustow, who was influenced by Oppenheimer, agreed that the "bloody deed of superstratification" gave birth to the State (38). But Rustow regarded a strict conquest theory as "an excessively narrow formulation," (7) though he did concede that the State usually arose during times of war and violence, even if it did not result directly from conquest. Similarly, the historian Fritz Kern regards Oppenheimer's thesis as "in need of much refinement, but, once so revised, contains a sound core." (7)

Edward Sait (133–4) questions Oppenheimer's account. If the peasants were miserable grubbers of the soil who were barely able to feed themselves, then we must wonder "why the rich herdsmen should wish to conquer the peasants, who, according to Oppenheimer's own description, had no surplus that would attract the cupidity of a plunderer." Sait (135) suggests that States had multiple origins, "arising independently among different peoples at different times."

Elman R. Service (270–3) is far more critical of Oppenheimer's account. Oppenheimer's thesis, he says, "found little support in anthropology." War is often found during the later stages of State development, but we cannot establish a simple causal relationship. Even when war was a significant factor, other conditions were required to establish a State. In such cases war was not so much a cause as one environmental factor among several.

The most serious problem with Oppenheimer's account is that his conquering herdsmen and conquered peasants appear to have been subjects of States that existed before the conquest. The conquerors, writes MacLeod (cited in Sait, 132), were merely "agents in the spread or diffusion of particular ancient forms of the state"; they extended the dominion of an existing State rather than creating a new one. Similarly, according to Elman Service, "the only instances we find of permanent subordination from war are when the government already exists." Morton Fried makes the same point and concludes: "rather than war and military roles being the source of stratification [i.e., the State], it seems that stratification is a provoker of war." (cited in Service, 271)

Oppenheimer responds to this line of criticism in an introduction written for the English translation of his book. It is self-evident, he argues, that even small groups of humans will have some kind of authority who functions as a judge and leader. "But this authority is not 'The State' in the sense in which I use the word." (il) If some choose to call any form of government or leadership the State, then Oppenheimer is unwilling to quibble over definitions. But to discuss this kind of State has no bearing on Oppenheimer's thesis. He contends that the sociological concept of the State refers to a definite historical phenomenon—an institution of political domination and economic exploitation—and this is the State that always originated in conquest. (il)

It is interesting to note that Oppenheimer also defends himself against the previous objection in his original text. He considers the possibility that victors and vanquished, previous to their merger into one State, might have previously belonged to separate States. (9) Oppenheimer meets this objection in a curious way; the concedes that "there is no method of obtaining historical proof to the contrary, since the beginnings of human history are unknown." (8) This means that history must render a verdict of "not proven" on Oppenheimer's conquest theory.

It seems that Oppenheimer, by his own admission, has failed, but actually he is just getting started. The inductive method of history is just one part of Oppenheimer's "philosophy of the State." Another part is the deductive method of economics; when this kind of reasoning is applied to the historical evidence, we must conclude with "absolute certainty that the State, as history shows it, the class State, could not have come about except through warlike subjection." (8)

Oppenheimer's economic argument centers around his refutation of the "law of primitive accumulation," i.e., the theory that attributes the origin of economic classes to a growing population that eventually acquired ownership of all arable land. This meant that latecomers had no choice but to hire themselves out to landowners—hence the origin of economic classes.

Oppenheimer's extensive refutation of this theory and its many variants does not appear in *The State*, but it is a crucial link in his deductive argument. Oppenheimer insists, as a matter of economic law, that a monopoly on land could not have been achieved through voluntary means, since there was plenty of arable land to go around; only conquest can explain the subjugation of large numbers of people and the emergence of a landless underclass of laborers. The primitive State that enforced this differentiation of classes is impossible to explain except through conquest and forced labor. Thus does Oppenheimer combine the deductive reasoning of economics with the inductive reasoning of history.

Oppenheimer's general methodology has a long and distinguished ancestry; this "theoretical" or "conjectural" history (as the Scottish philosopher Dugald Stewart called it) was used extensively by Adam Smith, David Hume and others in their school. Indeed, a primary function of spontaneous order theory (Smith's "invisible hand") was to explain the historical development of institutions in those case where concrete information is sorely lacking.

CONQUEST AND CONSENT

Whatever the historical origin of the State, the historical question is distinct from what political conclusions, if any, can be drawn from it. If the State originated in conquest or some other form of unjust violence (the "force theory," as I shall call it) this historical fact might seem to support libertarian conclusions. But this has proved the exception rather than the rule. The force theory, more often than not, has been used to establish anti-libertarian conclusions.

Let's assume, for the sake of argument, that all States originated in conquest or unjust violence. This force theory is then, at best, a plain historical fact; it does not "speak" or carry any hidden lessons. The facts of history must be interpreted with the aid of theory, and it is this theory that brings "meaning" to history.

Assuming the force theory to be true, what relevance does it have to the social contract argument? In 1739, David Hume remarked on a common piece of political wisdom:

> No maxim is more conformable, both to prudence and morals, than to submit quietly to the government, which we find established in the country where we happen to live, without enquiring too curiously into its origin and first establishment. Few governments will bear being examined so rigorously. (*Treatise* 558)

Some four decades later, shortly after the British had been defeated at Yorktown, the English Clergyman Josiah Tucker complained that this wise maxim of politics—"Not to be very inquisitive concerning the original Title of the reigning Powers" (85)—had been destroyed by John Locke and other defenders of natural rights, social contract, and revolution. The "Lockean System," according to Tucker, derived legitimate political power from consent, but this was a test that no real government could pass. Indeed, as Thomas Paine and other revolutionaries pointed out, European monarchies, far from originating in consent, arose from conquest and wholesale violence.

I cannot digress here to explain the problems in this position. Tucker distorted this part of the Lockean system, but this does not affect the main thrust of his critique. Tucker's major complaint was not against Locke's ideas, but against how the Americans used those ideas. The revolutionaries, Tucker believed, were mere hypocrites who used Locke's principles when they were useful, but later dropped them when they proved embarrassing.

Americans had accused the British of violating their rights by imposing taxes and other measures without the consent of colonial assemblies. But now, having kicked out British government, how would the victorious Americans go about setting up a new government? The Americans had cited Lockean principles in their effort to rid themselves of a government, but would they remain true to those same principles in their effort to establish a new government? Would those inalienable rights of man, which had been ravaged by the old system of government, remain pristine and sacred in the hands of the new government?

No, argued Tucker; this was an impossible task: "the Lockean System is an universal Demolisher of all Civil Governments, but not the Builder of any." (101) Did the victorious Americans give their citizens the choice of living in a state of nature without any government at all? No—this inconvenient bit of Lockean theory was simply ignored by the new rulers. The Americans were given only one choice: "Who should govern, *Americans* or *Englishmen*." (71) Neither the states nor the Continental Congress ruled by the consent of the people:

> Was any one of these Civil Governments at first formed, or is it now administered, and conducted according to the Lockean Plan? And did, or doth any of their Congresses, general or provincial, admit of that fundamental Maxim of Mr. Locke, that every Man has an *unalienable* Right to obey no other Laws, but those of his own making? No; no;—so far from it, that there are dreadful Fines and Confiscations, Imprisonments, and even Death made use of, as the only effectual Means for obtaining that Unanimity of Sentiment so much boasted of by these new-fangled Republicans, and so little practiced. (105)

Tucker's argument illustrates how theories of the origin of the State played a key role in the development of American revolutionary doctrine. These historical inquiries were not idle exercises, but serious business with explosive potential. When Franz Oppenheimer presented his "conquest theory" of the origin of the State, he simply added one more voice to an historical chorus.

As we have seen, Josiah Tucker argued that consent theory would deligitimate all existing governments, justify indiscriminate revolution, and land us in anarchy. Tucker was neither the first nor the last to raise the "specter of anarchy" in regard to social contract theory. Indeed, this criticism appeared decades before Locke—in the writings of Sir Robert Filmer, whose works, though not published until 1680, were written four decades earlier. Filmer is best known as John Locke's dead adversary, whose ragged defense of patriarchalism was thoroughly demolished by John Locke, James Tyrrell, and Algernon Sidney. Yet if Radical Whigs found easy pickings in Filmer's positive theories, they encountered serious problems when they tried to rebut his objections to Grotius, Bellarmine, and other carriers of consent theory.

Filmer repeatedly challenged consent theorists to explain why men would ever leave the anarchistic state of nature and voluntarily surrender their rights to government. Any philosopher who begins in a State of Nature is doomed to remain in that condition. We cannot use consent as a bootstrap to lift us out of anarchy, so consent is as unthinkable as anarchy itself.

As Filmer points out, natural rights can be alienated only by consent, so a government is legitimate only if it can trace its authority to the voluntary decisions of individuals. But this theory is historically absurd and theoretically implausible. No government has been established by contract, nor is there any reason why, given the natural right to freedom, any rational person would voluntarily subordinate his will and agree to be ruled by others.

Individual rights and natural liberty—these are the principles of anarchy, according to Filmer; they serve to justify resistance and revolution, but they can never serve as the foundation of government. Sovereignty is an all or nothing affair: there exists no middle ground between absolutism and anarchy.

This formidable argument ("Filmer's Challenge," as I call it) survived in the writings of David Hume, Adam Smith, Edmund Burke, Josiah Tucker, Jeremy Bentham, and other foes of consent theory.

It is in the writings of David Hume that we see Filmer's Challenge combined with a force theory of the State—thereby delivering a "one-two" punch to the midsection of consent theory from which it has never fully recovered. In his famous essay, "Of the Original Contract," Hume embraces a force theory of the origin of the State in no uncertain terms: "Almost all the governments, which exist at present, or of which there remains any record in story, have been founded originally, either in usurpation or conquest, or both, without any pretence of a fair consent, or voluntary subjection of the people." (*Essays* 471) Hume continues:

> It is vain to say, that all governments are or should be, at first, founded on popular consent, as much as the necessity of human affairs will admit. This favours entirely my pretension. I maintain, that human affairs will never admit of this consent; seldom the appearance of it. But that conquest or usurpation, that is, in plain terms, force, by dissolving the ancient governments, is the origin of almost all the new ones, which were ever established in the world. . . . [T]herefore, some other foundation of government must also be admitted. (*Essays* 473–4)

According to Hume, some people will always resist a new government, and these people must be forcibly suppressed. Over time, however, the government will assume an aura of legitimacy, and most people will obey as a matter of habit. It is therefore correct to say that people acquiesce to a government, but this should not be confused with consent. Consent is possible only where there is choice, and no government can permit obedience to become a matter of choice. Government, for Hume, is legitimate because it serves the "general interests or necessities of society." Consent has nothing to do with this.

Like Filmer before him, Hume fears that a consent theory will delegitimate all governments, justify indiscriminate revolution, and so lead to "the disorders which attend all revolutions and changes of government." (*Essays* 486) Consent theory leads to a condition of anarchy—and this alone is sufficient to condemn it. Indeed, "nothing is clearer proof, that a theory of this kind is erroneous, than to find, that it leads to paradoxes, repugnant to the common sentiments of mankind, and to the practice and opinion of all nations and all ages." (ibid.)

This *reductio* demolition of consent theory was elevated to an art form in 1756 (eight years after the publication of Hume's essay) by a young Edmund Burke. In *A Vindication of Natural Society*, Burke presents himself as an anonymous champion of consent theory who argues passionately against the violence, wars, and other brutalities of governments. Governments originate in conquest and violence—"All empires have been cemented in blood." (50) Thus, according to the "sure and uncontested principles" of that "great philosopher," Mr. Locke, "the greatest part of the governments on earth must be concluded tyrannies, impostures, violations of the natural rights of mankind, and worse than the most disorderly anarchies." (53)

Burke, of course, intended this as satire; by embracing the anarchistic *reductio* of consent theory, he hoped to show its absurdity. But Burke's *Vindication* was so convincing that many took it seriously, thus making it the first modern defense of anarchism. In 1765, as Burke thought of entering Parliament, he wanted to remove all doubt about his satire, so he prefaced the second edition with a disclaimer: his *Vindication* was nothing more than a lesson in "the abuse of reason" as practiced by consent theorists—those who live in the "fairyland of philosophy."

Despite its satirical intent, Burke's *Vindication* presents a compelling historical case for the coercive origin of the State. Burke uses this data to dismiss consent theory, but the same data might be used to dismiss the State. This is precisely what we find in William Godwin's *Enquiry Concerning Political Justice* (1793)—the first comprehensive defense of philosophic anarchism.

Godwin's treatment of the origin of the State is merely a summary of the material contained in Burke's *Vindication*. Godwin agrees with Hume, Burke and others that governments can never be made to conform with consent theory. But where others fled from the anarchistic *reductio* of consent theory, Godwin embraced it. If government cannot be based on consent, then so much the worse for government.

From the above considerations we can see the importance and power of the conquest theory of the State. Although it is not possible to argue directly from the fact that States originated in conquest to their lack of justification, the conquest theory does block the most popular method of justifying the present State: consent theory. If the State originated in conquest and usurpation, it is clear that its citizens, those who are exploited by those who control the political machinery of the State, *did* not, and *would* not, consent to be so exploited. Consent, whether actual or tacit, ceases to be a plausible way of justifying the State.

I am glad to see Oppenheimer's classic back in print—notwithstanding his optimistic conclusions—for he gives lovers of liberty everywhere a powerful tool with which to shake up the "common sense" and "received wisdom" of mankind.

George H. Smith
San Francisco
July 1995

George H. Smith is the author of *Atheism: The Case Against God*; *Atheism, Ayn Rand, and Other Heresies*; and numerous articles on various aspects of libertarianism.

NOTES

1. Page numbers refer to this edition of *The State*.
2. The Marxian approach, like that of Oppenheimer, is frequently placed in the "conflict school" of sociology, but with this difference: the former upholds a theory of the State based on "internal conflict" (i.e., of classes), whereas the latter is a theory of "external conflict." Proponents of "external conflict" believe that the State emerged from the conflict and forcible merger of two groups, victors and vanquished, which had formerly existed as separate communities. (This is the modern "conquest theory" of the origin of the State.)

WORKS REFERENCED

Bodin, Jean. *Six Books of the Commonwealth*. Abridged and translated by M. J. Tooley. Oxford: Basil Blackwell, 1955.

Burke, Edmund. *A Vindication of Natural Society* in *Selected Writings and Speeches*. Edited by Peter J. Stanlis. Gloucester, Mass.: Peter Smith, 1968.

Filmer, Sir Robert. *Patriarcha and Other Works*. Edited by Peter Laslett. Oxford: Basil Blackwell, 1949.

Gumplowicz, Ludwig. *Outlines of Sociology*. Edited by Irving L. Horowitz. New York: Paine-Whitman Publishers, 1963.

Hume, David. *A Treatise of Human Nature*. Edited by L. A. Selby-Bigge, Second Edition revised by P. H. Hidditch. Oxford: Oxford University Press, 1978.

———— *Essays: Moral, Political, and Literary*. Edited by Eugene F. Miller. Indianapolis: Liberty Fund, 1987.

Kern, Fritz. *Kingship and Law in the Middle Ages*. Translated by S. B. Chrimes. New York: HarperCollins, 1956.

Pascal, Blaise. *Pascal's Pensées*. Translated by W. F. Trotter. London: J. M. Dent & Sons Ltd., 1932.

Rustow, Alexander. *Freedom and Domination*. Translated by Salvator Attanasio. Princeton: Princeton University Press, 1980.

Sait, Edward. *Political Institutions: A Preface*. New York: Appleton, 1938.

Service, Elman. *Origins of the State and Civilization: The Progress of Cultural Evolution*. New York: W. W. Norton & Co., 1975.

Tocqueville, Alexis de. *The Old Regime and the French Revolution*. Translated by Stuart Gilbert. New York: Doubleday, 1955.

Tucker, Josiah. *A Treatise Concerning Civil Government* (1781). Reprint New York: Augustus Kelley, 1967.

Turgot, Anne-Robert-Jacques. *On Universal History* in *Turgot on Progress, Sociology and Economics*. Translated, edited and with an introduction by Ronald L. Meek. Cambridge: Cambridge University Press, 1973.

Weber, Max. *Economy and Society: An Outline of Interpretive Sociology*. Vol. 1, edited by Guenther Roth and Claus Wittich. New York: Bedminister Press, 1968.

INTRODUCTION TO THE FREE LIFE EDITION

A small minority has stolen the heritage of humanity.—Franz Oppenheimer

The State is a condition, a certain relationship between human beings, a mode of human behavior; we destroy it by contracting other relationships, by behaving differently.—Gustav Landauer

The State affects the most mundane as well as the most important aspects of our lives. As a powerful, sprawling institution it shapes the other major institutions of our society and reaches into our most personal everyday affairs. As Robert Nisbet has written, "the single most decisive influence upon Western social organization has been the rise and development of the centralized territorial state."[1]

But, surprisingly, little of importance has been written on the State. In fact, a quick review of the books and articles reveals that most of them have been largely rationalizations of the coercion and force that all States practice. Such diverse people as George Sabine (a quite traditional political scientist) and Robert P. Wolff (a more radical and questioning political philosopher) have made this point.[2]

One exception to this tendency to rationalize is *The State* by Franz Oppenheimer. In this classic, he presents a strongly libertarian view of the State. He neither defends it nor condemns it out of hand. Rather, through his study of history and political economy, he seeks to understand its nature and development. His work leads him to conclude that:

> The State, completely in its genesis, essentially and almost completely during the first stages of its existence, is a social institution, forced by a victorious group of men on a defeated group, with the sole purpose of regulating the dominion of the victorious group over the vanquished, and securing itself against revolt from within and attacks from abroad. Teleologically, this dominion had no other purpose than the economic exploitation of the vanquished by the victors.[3]

This may seem somewhat polemical, but I think he is essentially correct. I hope that this short introduction and especially the book itself, will reintroduce Oppenheimer's conquest theory of the State and prove suggestive to others studying the State.

There is very little in English on Franz Oppenheimer's intellectual and, for that matter, political development.[4] He was the most Western-minded of the early German sociologists, rejecting racial interpretations of history while championing a Proudhonian ideal of a truly free society.[5] But Oppenheimer did fall squarely within a German sociological tradition and he was one of its more important thinkers.

Sociology came to Germany at the beginning of this century. Rooted as it was in history, philosophy and political economy, sociology did not dissipate its energy in statistical minutiae and obscure topics. Reminiscent of Comte and Spencer, early German sociology was involved in the grand sweep of history and social life.

It is not surprising then that one of the first "schools" of German sociology was historical sociology. Oppenheimer certainly fit under that rubric, along with people like Alfred Weber, Karl Mannheim, Max Scheler and Max Weber. Concerned with "depicting individual instances," with "interpreting historical evolution," and with "collective realities" (culture and the State, for instance), they wrote in large strokes for the insight it gave into current life.

> Sociology is conceived as being akin to a theory of universal history and as undertaking the tasks of the philosophy of history; namely, the provision of an answer to present anxieties out of the experience of the past.[6]

They also wrote with a clear and profound understanding of the crucial role played by conflict in every area of social life: hence, the importance of conflict theory for this group. The two greatest names in historical sociology are Karl Marx and Max Weber. Marx preceded the development of historical sociology as a distinct school and set the tone on a number of important points. As Randall Collins outlines it:

> He brought together for the first time the major sources of the conflict tradition: the revelations of historical scholarship, the effort at a materialist theory of society, the iconoclasm of the freethinkers.[7]

Of particular importance was Marx's emphasis on the material preconditions of human action and the importance of material factors in shaping human action (without, it should be noted, denying the crucial importance of thinking as an activity by human actors). This grounded philosophy in history and was an effective attack on pure idealism.

Max Weber was without a doubt one of the greatest sociologists and thinkers of recent times. Weber and Oppenheimer were contemporaries both in time and in intellectual pursuits. They were both deeply affected by Marx and clearly immersed in historical and empirical work. Randall Collins includes them all as thinkers in the tradition of the conflict theory. Weber and Oppenheimer, however, emphasized a different set of problems than did Marx, and developed a different theory. While Collins rightly includes Marx in his discussion of conflict theory, Anthony Giddens is more correct when he emphasizes the importance of domination and subordination:

> Oversimplifying somewhat, it might be said that Weber gives to the organization of relationships of domination and subordination the prominence which Marx attributes to relationships of production.[8]

In either case conflict is one of the important underpinnings of historical sociology.

> The central focus is on the organization of material arrangements into a system of power which divides society into interest groups struggling for control.[9]

This dynamic of struggle and how it is handled offers a way of explaining the entire social structure so well that Randall Collins contends "that conflict theory has been vindicated by empirical evidence to an extent approached by no other sociological theory."[10] This view of the dynamic of conflict is not new. Not taking into account the political use to which this insight was put, the idea is evident in the Epicureans, in Ibn Khaldun, Machiavelli, Voltaire, Hobbes, Hume, Spencer and Lester Ward. Their ideas and the indigenous conflict theories of Ludwig Gumplowicz (who Oppenheimer acknowledges was very influential on his own thinking) and Gustav Ratzenhofer set the stage for the writings on conflict theory in this century.[11]

Oppenheimer's emphasis, in the book at hand, is the State and its origin and development. It represents a major contribution to the theories of conflict and conquest. But who was Franz Oppenheimer?

Franz Oppenheimer was born in a suburb of Berlin on March 30, 1864. He became a physician in 1885, and practiced medicine for a decade. He was aware of and quite concerned about the social issues of his time and he became acquainted with many of the radical movements: the marxists and revisionists, the liberal socialists and land nationalizers, the federalists and anarchists. Influenced by all of these and yet not convinced by any, he went back to school in economics. He supported his wife and child by writing articles. In 1908, at the age of 44, he received his Ph.D. at the University of Kiel. The next year he became a *privatdozent* (unsalaried lecturer receiving only student's fees) of economics at the University of Berlin. During these years he was very involved in the cooperative and back-to-the-land movements that were common then.

During the First World War he was an economic counselor in the War Office. In 1919 he became *ordinarius* (full professor) of economics and sociology at the University of Frankfort. Ill-health forced him to retire in 1929 at the age of 65 (his chair, incidentally, was taken by Karl Mannheim). For the next four years he lived at a rural cooperative settlement near Berlin that he had helped form prior to World War I.

In 1933 Oppenheimer left Germany and taught in France and Palestine and then came to the United States. He continued to write and in 1941 was a founding editor of the *American Journal of Economics and Sociology*, a journal which followed the ideas of Henry George. He died in Los Angeles on September 30, 1943.

Oppenheimer always contended that the social sciences would affirm and support the search for justice. He combined his scholarship with a reforming zeal "which sometimes becomes an obsession [calling] forth alternately respect and irritation."[12] As Eduard Heimann said:

> He was a liberal of that old, heroic, revolutionary brand which has otherwise died out long ago. . . . Oppenheimer calls himself a liberal socialist. He is a socialist in that he regards capitalism as a system of exploitation, and capital revenue as the gain of that exploitation, but a liberal in that he believes in the harmony of a genuinely free market.[13]

In an article published after his death, Oppenheimer set down his long held belief that there is an alternative to the totalitarianism of Fascism and Bolshevism and the exploitation of the current amalgam of political democracy, which isn't democracy at all, and capitalism, which is really just "the bastard offspring of slavery and freedom."[14]

> There is a third possibility: a perfect democracy, not only *politically* but also *economically*. . . . The first condition of perfect democracy is equal opportunity for all, or, which is the same, free untrammeled competition.[15]

That equal opportunity and free untrammeled competition seem so contradictory is indicative of the fact that we may still not have come to realize that "perfect democracy" *is* an alternative. But Oppenheimer believed that history and empirical work would prove these points.

> It is the task of social science, especially of theoretical economics, to teach this gospel [of freedom] and spread the conviction that perfect democracy is more than a daydream of some utopianist outsiders.[16]

From 1893 until his death in 1943, Oppenheimer wrote hundreds of books, pamphlets, articles and reviews.[17] These ran the gamut from economic theory to polemics about the major intellectual strains of his day. Very little of his major work is in English. His most important work is the four double-volumes of the *System of Sociology*. In 4,500 pages Oppenheimer constructed a theory of general sociology and social psychology (Volume I), political theory (II), economic theory (III), and economic and social history (IV). One review referred to it as "by far the most elaborate system of sociology ever written."[18] Yet it is ironic that only an early, sketchy version of volume two has ever been translated into English: *The State*. Sketchy though it may be, there is much of interest and importance in it.

Positions of leadership are not much coveted by the Ik. They are backed by little power, and in so far as they confer any benefits (i.e., *ngag,* or food) upon the of officeholder, that only serves to make him all the more edible.—Colin Turnbull in *The Mountain People*

There are many ways to look at the State. Since the early Greek philosophers there has been a tendency to view it as the ideal and/or the only important form of social organization.[19] The State is given a pre-eminence and a universality that betrays a massive bias in favor of the State.

Some, like E. Adamson Hoebel, think that "where there is political organization there is a state. If political organization is universal, so then is the state."[20] This view dilutes any meaning the State might have. Others try to be rid of the concept altogether, an approach exemplified by the functionalists. Gabriel Almond and James Coleman feel that the "rejection of the 'state and non–state' classification . . . is a matter of theoretical and operational importance. . . . If the functions are there then the structures must be."[21] It does seem naive however to assume that any function must be met by a similar structure. In that case, we are confronted by an undifferentiated mass of information about different cultures and social institutions that can't be meaningfully discussed.

Oppenheimer, on the other hand, correctly appreciates the State's crucial importance, but he *also* emphasizes its distinctiveness. He does this by developing the distinction between the economic means and the political means. This is one of Oppenheimer's most important contributions.

To talk about the economic and the political *means* is Oppenheimer's way of emphasizing the actions and processes by which people seek to satisfy their common needs for material sustenance. There are two basic organizing principles of social life. One is essentially peaceful and is what Oppenheimer calls the economic means: "one's own labor and the equivalent exchange of one's own labor for the labor of others." Life is based on peaceful existence, equality of opportunity and voluntary exchange. The other is the political means, which is based on domination and is essentially violent: "the unrequited appropriation of the labor of others."[22]

The difference between the political and the economic means is similar to the probably better known distinction between State and society.[23] In fact, Oppenheimer calls the State the "organization of the political means." However, Oppenheimer's choice of words constantly reminds us of the action and process involved in the distinctions. "Society," for instance, is often seen as a static and monolithic term. It is not; nor is it some integrated whole as the functionalists, among others, suggest. It is, rather, a vast and fluid network of individuals and groups that interact voluntarily on the basis of shared economic interests or on the basis of feelings of identity and community. This is the economic means at work. It is unfortunate that we have become so jaded that we cannot see the effectiveness and importance of these voluntary interactions in our daily lives and in the larger social order.[24]

In earlier times this voluntary interaction was called "natural society." It is in a real sense prior to the State. In fact it can be said that the State develops out of society as a secondary formation and is "the alienated form of society,"[25] serving the interests of social classes unequally.

The State rises out of society when some people utilize the political means for their own advantage. Some individuals or groups are in a position to enforce actions upon others and by others. Relations become based on super- and sub-ordination. The State then "is first of all an apparatus of domination."[26]

This distinction between the economic means and the political means or society and State is a powerful tool in understanding the world that has passed us and the world around us. While the two in fact flow into one another, at times, they are essentially separate and this should be constantly kept in mind. As Reinhard Bendix says in his article on "Social Stratification and the Political Community":

> The distinction refers to a universal attribute of group life in the sense that, however interrelated, these two types of human association are not reducible to each other. From an analytical viewpoint it is necessary to consider "society" and "the state" as interdependent, but autonomous spheres of thought and action which coexist in one form or another in all complex societies.[27]

This distinction between the two means of coordination is not merely an analytic nicety. In an admittedly simplified form it is the major dynamic of history, "the basic social struggle in human history."[28]

We see the voluntary cooperation of the economic means every day, from our own personal friendships to the small-scale exchange of goods and services between individuals.[29] But there have also been cases where these voluntary means were virtually the sole mechanism of coordination among groups of people. Often considered primitive by our patronizing language of progress, they were quite extraordinary societies. The study of these Stateless societies (as they have come to be called) is important and interesting precisely because "one of the most essential things that we can learn from the life of rude tribes is how society can function without the policeman to keep order."[30] Studying Stateless societies gives us a better perspective on the uses of the economic means and on those societies which *have* States.

Any group of people have to interact and that means some form of coordination must be effected. As we have seen, cooperation and domination are these ways. Within such a group there will also arise moments of conflict, and they must be mediated and resolved in some way. There is a view which holds that the minimal domain of the State is the protection and the provision of justice. Such a position is untenable in view of the numerous ways conflicts are resolved without the State. Stateless societies are important precisely because they show that non-State resolutions of conflict can encompass large social groups and continue for some time.

Stateless societies include many dissimilar types. It is only necessary to define them in a general way here. Stateless societies

> have few or no roles whose primarily goal is the exercise of authority. Authority and political action there are, but they are exercised through multipurpose roles in which they cannot be said to form the primary element.[31]

Stateless societies are not just a few geographically restricted and primitive societies. Most of the evidence is about primitive societies but this says more about the imperialistic nature of States than it does about the limitations of Stateless societies. There is no inherent reason why we can not have and can not work for a Stateless society in our own time. Some of these societies have included the Kung Bushmen of South Africa and the African Logoli, the Tallinsi and the Nuer, the Eskimos, the Ifugao of the Philippines and the Star Mountain people of New Guinea.[32] They have ranged from patrilineal to matrilineal and from pastoral to hunting. They have lived nomadically, in villages or confederacies. In fact, until conquered by the Europeans, State organizations were *exceptional* in Oceania, sub-Saharan Africa and the Americas.[33]

It is held that the State is necessary for the integration of society. The modern State provides "a uniquely effective form of social integration."[34] Indeed, terrifyingly effective! Compare this to the "remarkable spectacle of societies positively maintaining themselves at a high level of integration without any obvious specialized means of enforcement. . . ."[35] We may say then that Stateless societies achieve the same ends as States but through vastly different means.[36] Aidan Southall sums this up beautifully when he says:

Stateless societies are so constituted that the kaleidoscopic succession of concrete social situations provides the stimulus that motivates each individual to act for his own interest or for that of close kin and neighbors with whom he is so totally involved, in a manner which maintains the fabric of society. It is a little like the classical model of laissez-faire economics translated into the political field . . . the lack of specialized roles and the resulting multiplex quality of social networks mean that neither economic nor political ends can be exclusively pursued by anyone to the detriment of society, because the ends are intertwined with each other and further channeled by ritual and controlled by the beliefs which ritual expresses.[37]

We need not look solely to so-called primitive societies for examples of Stateless societies. Germany in the early middle ages "was in some ways the complete antithesis of the modern state."[38] Until the seventeenth century, Ireland had "no legislature, no bailiffs, no police, no public enforcement of justice. . . . There was no trace of State-administered justice."[39] And in early America there were notable attempts to forge something anarchistic. Murray Rothbard has mentioned Albemarle, Rhode Island and Pennsylvania.[40]

The point is not to suggest that the Stateless and near Stateless societies which have existed were in any way perfect. They were not, but they did exist and they did attempt to solve social problems in a way different from the usual reliance on force, centralization and the political means. Stateless societies have been remarkably viable.

Since his interest was specifically on the State, Oppenheimer spent no time on this larger discussion of the economic means and Stateless societies. We have mentioned such societies because they suggest a breadth to the significance of the economic means.

Taking the State wherever found, striking into its history at any point, one sees no way to differentiate the activities of its founders, administrators, and beneficiaries from those of a professional-criminal class.—Albert Jay Nock

The first task Oppenheimer set himself was to trace the origins of the State. He saw the State rising out of conflict and out of the conquest of one group by another. Let us put this in context by briefly discussing other theories of the State.

The usual view of the origin of the State (when it is discussed at all) is that it rose spontaneously and naturally. People voluntarily gave up their sovereignty. This is known as the Social Contract, a convenient metaphor. It is an implausible theory and there is just no proof that such a thing ever really happened.

Others see the State rising rather naturally from economic surplus and the division of labor. R. H. Lowie and R. M. MacIver see the State as one association (albeit the most powerful) out of many that make up the larger society.[41] While there is a definite validity to economic differentiation and the State-like possibilities of primitive associations, they do not, as Oppenheimer would be quick to point out, cause or lead naturally to the State. There is no discussion of what exactly would propel differentiation or association into the State.

Another view of the rise of the State sees the propelling force in the imperatives of technological centralization. This was most forcefully presented by Karl Wittfogel in his study of oriental despotisms.[42] For him the material needs of an area and the solution (specifically large-scale irrigation) led to the formation of a central political unit: the State. While irrigation projects did significantly strengthen the State, they did not bring about its formation. As Jacques Gernet has pointed out:

> historically, it was the pre-existing state structures and the large, well trained labor force provided by the armies that made the great irrigation projects possible.[43]

Furthermore, it is not clearly the case that the solutions to certain problems (that is to make progress in civilization) must come *a priori* out of or result in technological centralization. Clearly there is something else at work.[44]

This brings us to the conflict theory of the origins of the State.[45] For as important as these previous theories are, they can not account for the "jump" from non-State to State. For Oppenheimer this rests on the point where the voluntarism of the economic means is subsumed under concerted and continuous use of the political means:

> A close examination of history indicates that only a coercive theory can account for the rise of the state. Force, and not enlightened self-interest, is the mechanism by which political evolution has led, step by step, from autonomous villages to the state.[46]

The State rises out of a condition of Statelessness or "practical anarchy." In general, these are essentially societies of equals and there are no roles of authority and little social or economic differentiation. Certain economic inequalities do arise through luck, cleverness, etc. Oppenheimer explicitly recognizes these economic inequalities among herdsmen as an element of Statehood. However, because of his Georgist view of the importance of land and his understanding of the dynamics of the economic means, he sees a tendency for these inequalities to remain modest and to be resolved. The condition of relative equality will be approximately restored. Thus, while he sees that differentiation can and does arise through economic means, he explicitly rejects that it is this primitive accumulation which results in the State.[47]

This condition of relative equality is permanently destroyed by the use of the political means by one group against another in the form of war or raiding. For Oppenheimer, the State rises through conquest. In fact

> No primitive State known to history originated in any other manner. . . .
> Everywhere we find some warlike tribe of wild men breaking through
> the boundaries of some less warlike people, settling down as nobility and
> founding the State.[48]

Oppenheimer proceeds to mention examples from around the world. Lawrence Krader has more recently pointed out, "There is no doubt that conquest played a part in most if not all processes of state formation."[49]

It is conquest, then, of one group by another that leads directly to the State. While this is a striking and important insight, it can not really be considered sufficient.

> The conquest theory failed as a general theory of the origin of the state
> because it introduced only external factors and failed to take into account
> internal processes. . . .[50]

It would be helpful, then, to go back to the beginnings of economic differentiation and take another look at how conflict and the political means enter into the process of State-formation.

Morton Fried goes considerably beyond Oppenheimer in his discussion of inequality as a germ of Statehood. In his discussion of the evolution of political society, he sees it going through stages from an egalitarian to a ranking to a stratified society. Society is still basically

Stateless at this point. In the latter case, access to basic resources is limited and there is clear economic differentiation. But rather than saying, as Oppenheimer does, that this situation will resolve itself back towards equality, Fried makes the point that stratification is unstable and must change—there are two possibilities:

> The state forms in embryo in the stratified society, which, by this reasoning, must be one of the least stable models of organization that has ever existed. The stratified society is torn between two possibilities: It builds within itself great pressures for its own dissolution and for a return to a simpler kind of organization, either of ranking or egalitarian kind. . . . On the other side, the stratified community, to maintain itself, must evolve more powerful institutions of political control than ever were called upon to maintain a system of differential ranking.[51]

Within this instability there are movements toward equality and the economic means and movements in the direction of the political means whereby some seek to rigidify their economic gains. However, the outcome seems depressingly clear according to Oppenheimer, that "wherever opportunity offers, and man possesses the power, he prefers political to economic means for the preservation of his life."[52]

As the use of the political means of robbery and expropriation becomes more frequent and institutionalized, the State takes shape. *Internally*, although Oppenheimer is not concerned with this, war (or raids) leads to the centralization of the warring group. As Georg Simmel said, "war needs a centralistic intensification of the group form, and this is guaranteed best by despotism."[53]

In fact there is some evidence that defense against external conquest led to the development of the State in Ancient Sumer.[54] Booty from such wars certainly solidified class differentiation within an already hierarchical form. Randolph Bourne's insightful comment that "War is the health of the State" certainly is true, even in our own time.[55]

Externally, which is Oppenheimer's emphasis, the political means leads to the conquest of one group by another and to the genesis of the State. Oppenheimer distinguishes six stages in this process.

The first stage involves continuous raiding and killing between groups. But it is the second stage that exhibits two necessary elements that make the giant step from robbery to State robbery. The peasants cease to resist these incursions. They accept their fate and their subservience. The herdsmen no longer merely loot, rape and kill, though such violence is continued to the extent necessary to insure acquiescence; now they appropriate the surplus of the peasants, leaving enough for the peasants to continue producing so that the herdsmen may skim the top off the next harvest also.

> The moment when first the conqueror spared his victim in order permanently to exploit him in productive work, was of incomparable historical importance. It gave birth to nation and State, to right and the higher economics, with all the developments and ramifications which have grown and which will hereafter grow out of them.[56]

Out of this "arrangement" comes the beginning of the process of integration whereby both master and "slave" recognize certain common interests and their common humanity. Customary rights begin to develop into the first threads of jural relations. Even though this internal development begins and legal rights and wrongs become defined, it is important to keep in mind that these develop within the context of class interests and for class interests.

The third stage arrives when the peasants regularly bring their surplus as tribute. This is the beginning of taxation.

The next stage in the genesis of the State comes with the territorial union of the two groups. This allows the ruling group to "protect" its subjects and its economic base from external incursions. But it also permits the ruling group to better oversee internal affairs and smash uprisings against its hegemony.

In the fifth stage, the rulers assume the right to arbitrate. Thus the judicial function is taken out of the local and common law context. This gives the rulers much greater control to enforce their own interests and to mediate conflicts.

Finally the primitive State is complete. The last stage is the need to

> develop the habit of rule and the usages of government. The two groups, separated to begin with, and then united on one territory, are at first merely laid alongside one another, then are scattered through one another . . . soon the bonds of relationship unite the upper and the lower strata.[57]

These stages, which Oppenheimer describes, are analytically useful. But Oppenheimer did not mean to have them rigidly regarded. Some States have developed through these stages; others, however, have skipped or combined stages. In any case, the State is formed.

The State then is the organization of the political means. The State "can have originated in no other way than through conquest and subjugation."[58] For Oppenheimer, every State in history has been a State of classes; that is a polity of superior and inferior social groups, based upon distinctions either of rank or of property. The master or ruling class tries to maintain the "law of the political means" and is thereby conservative and even reactionary. The subject or the ruled class wants to substitute the "law of equality" for all inhabitants of the State, which makes for liberalism and revolution.

His emphasis on class, on the distinction between rulers and ruled, has led some observers, like R. H. Lowie, to claim that Oppenheimer's theory

> is properly not a theory of the State but a theory of caste. It explains the origin of hereditary classes, but it does not solve the more fundamental problem of all political organization. . . . Conquest led to complication and integration, but the germs of statehood antedated these processes.[59]

Of course, as we have seen, Oppenheimer agrees that the germs of Statehood were there, but it was only with concerted use of the political means, the conquest of one group by another, that led to the actual formation of the State. While other factors are also involved, the State always retains its class characteristics.

Once Oppenheimer had made the distinction between the economic means and the political means, described the genesis of the State and indicated its basic nature in the political means, conquest and class, he proceeded to outline the State's further development. Oppenheimer's own discussion of this is itself very short and often borders on the metaphorical. But there is significant material there. It is important to point out a few of the major points.

Whatever the further developments of the State are, Oppenheimer constantly repeats that its basic form and nature do not change. From the primitive feudal State through the modern constitutional State, it is still the institutionalization of the political means by one class to expropriate the economic wealth of another.

The development of the State beginning with the primitive feudal State brought two internal developments which had opposite directions: first, a continuing process of social integration, of breaking down the separate cultures of various groups within the State; and second, a process of social differentiation along class lines leading to class-consciousness.

A whole series of processes, ranging from the assimilation of languages and religions to intermarriage, lead to a "spirit of fraternity and of equity." Ethnic differences and the mere recognition of physical boundaries produce a "them" and "us" mentality, along with a feeling of group solidarity. And internally, "A far stronger bond of psychical community between high and low . . . is woven by legal protection against the aggression of the mighty." This is "a consciousness of belonging to the State."[60]

This pulling together is opposed by a pulling apart that is just as powerful. This is the development of class consciousness among both the upper strata (rulers) and the lower strata (ruled). Class consciousness through the development of class theories is the psychological dynamic in history, just as economic needs is the material dynamic. As the process of State consciousness proceeds, a class theory of the ruling group becomes necessary to direct, modify and sustain the State. Although approached from a somewhat different angle, this crucial point is admitted by most political philosophers.

> As soon, however, as the psychic integration develops, in any degree, the community feeling of State consciousness, as soon as the bond servant acquires "rights," and the consciousness of essential equality percolates through the mass, the political means requires a system of justification; and there arises in the ruling class the group theory of "legitimacy."[61]

All questions of State legitimacy, then, can only be founded on or traced back to class and class theories. As Morton Fried so succinctly put it, "Legitimacy, no matter how its definition is phrased, is the means by which ideology is blended with power."[62]

The final stage in the State's development is what Oppenheimer calls the modern constitutional State. This is the most sophisticated level because domination and exploitation continue but are limited by public law and hidden by a complex ideological superstructure. As Oppenheimer says:

> Its *form* still continues to be domination, its content still remains the exploitation of the economic means. The latter continues to be limited by public law, which on the one hand protects the traditional "distribution" of the total products of the nation; while on the other it attempts to maintain at their full efficiency the taxpayers and those bound

to render service. The internal policy of the State continues to revolve in the path prescribed for it by the parallelogram of the centrifugal force of class contests and the centripetal impulse of the common interests in the State; and its foreign policy continues to be determined by the interests of the master class, now comprising besides the landed also the moneyed interests.[63]

It should be clear by now that in addition to the sameness that the State exhibits throughout all its stages, Oppenheimer also sees a steady progress in the State's development. This assumption of the inevitability of progress is problematic as there is little basis for believing it in this day and age. But for Oppenheimer it meant that the State culminated in what he called the freemen's citizenship. In his last chapter he makes it clear that the State of the future will be society guided by self-govern-ment.[64] Even though the State rises out of the political means and conquest, and is a class State, Oppenheimer sees the economic means eventually predominating and the class State disappearing. Oppenheimer, however, is no anarchist. He was, as we have men-tioned, quite the classical liberal.

> No great society can exist without a body which renders final decisions on debatable issues and has the means, in case of emergency, to enforce decisions. No society can exist without the power of punishment of the judge, nor without the right to expropriate property even against the wish of the proprietor, if the public interest demands it.[65]

Once the domination and administration of the ruling class and the economic monopoly of the land are removed from the class State, then we would have, according to Oppenheimer, a truly free society (perhaps a class-less State).

> In such a society all political power would lie in the base of the pyramid: in the communitives [sic] and cooperatives. While the administrators on top, as I once wrote, would only have a power comparable let us say, to the one of the international geodetic committee.[66]

When the class-less society is reached it would rest in a steady state. For similar to his discussion of primitive accumulation earlier, he sees that it would be "impossible for any abuse of power to be introduced beyond the simple level of individual theft, which would be swiftly punished."[67]

It is certainly shocking and unsettling to read his conclusion. After a sustained and remarkable discussion of the State as oppressive and class-oriented, it is difficult to see how we will be rather miraculously presented with a society somewhere between the anarchist ideal of free collectives and the classical liberal ideal of a neutral State. Certainly everything Oppenheimer has said and taught us shows the neutral State as contradictory. As C. J. Friedrich said years ago, "The 'state' as some kind of neutral god charged with looking after the national interest is so central in all dictatorial ideologies . . ."[68] This may be a little hard on Oppenheimer but it certainly is to the point.

Part of the context for Oppenheimer's conclusion can be seen in the contrasts between the sociological optimism and pessimism of his day. The pessimists accepted the rise of the State and totalitarianism with either glee or regret. Those who were part of the ruled class saw, then, revolution as the only solution. This would, in Oppenheimer's eyes, cause more problems than it would solve. He, on the other hand, was an optimist and his reading of history and political economy showed him that the class State would indeed *evolve* into a class-less State. He was one of the small fraction of social liberals, or liberal Socialists who

> believe in the evolution of a society without class dominion and class exploitation which will guarantee to the individual, besides political, also economic liberty of movement, within of course the limitations of the economic means. That was the credo of the old social liberalism of pre-Manchester days, enunciated by Quesnay and especially by Adam Smith, and again taken up in modern times by Henry George and Theodore Hertzka.[69]

While his optimism and belief in evolution may be misplaced for us who live in an increasingly centralized and politicized world, Oppenheimer's analysis can be very helpful as we try to understand and change our world.

Oppenheimer's optimistic conclusion that States will necessarily give way to what he termed freemen's citizenship seems much less certain to us today. In a world dominated by war and the authoritarian State, our sense of inevitable progress has been shaken.

Oppenheimer's historical discussion of the origins and rise of the State, however, is clearly very relevant. The element of conflict and conquest has played a part in the origins of most States. Together with the emphasis on the use of the political means and the class nature of the State's interests, we can begin to see history a little differently. No longer can we say that States are benign in the process of history.

Any further judgement on the significance of *The State* can be made by the reader. Whatever its relevance, Oppenheimer believed that the social sciences were important precisely to the extent that they valued and tried to extend human life and freedom.

Charles Hamilton
Crompond, N.Y.
May 1975

Charles Hamilton was President and Editor-in-Chief of Free Life Editions. He has subsequently edited collections by and about Frank Chodorov, Benjamin Tucker, and Albert Jay Nock. He has been editor of *The Freeman*, and Director of Publications and a Program Officer at Liberty Fund.

NOTES

1. Robert A. Nisbet, *Community and Power* (London: Oxford University Press, 1962), p. 98.

2. George Sabine, "State," *Encyclopedia of the Social Sciences*, vol. 14 (New York: Macmillan, 1934), p. 331, and Robert Paul Wolff, *In Defense of Anarchism* (New York: Harper & Row, 1970), pp. 5, 8, 9.

3. Franz Oppenheimer, *The State*, p. 9. All page references to *The State* refer to this edition of the book.

4. Paul Honigsheim's article is suggestive of some of these influences. "The Sociological Doctrines of Franz Oppenheimer: An Agrarian Philosophy of History and Social Reform," Harry Elmer Barnes, ed., *An Introduction to the History of Sociology* (Chicago: University of Chicago Press, 1948), pp. 332–352.

5. Raymond Aron, *German Sociology* (New York: Free Press, 1964), p. 43.

6. Ibid., p. 37.

7. Randall Collins, "Reassessments of Sociological History: The Empirical Validity of the Conflict Tradition," *Theory and Society*, Summer 1974, p. 159.

8. Anthony Giddens, *Capitalism and Modern Social Theory* (London: Cambridge University Press, 1971), p. 234.

9. Randall Collins, op. cit., p. 174.

10. Ibid., pp. 150–51.

11. See Howard Becker and Harry Elmer Barnes, *Social Thought from Lore to Science* (New York: Dover, 1961) for information on some early proponents of the conflict theory. See especially pp. 702–734.

12. Raymond Aron, op. cit., p. 43.

13. Eduard Heimann, "Franz Oppenheimer's Economic Ideas," *Social Research*, vol. II, no. 1, Feb. 1944, pp. 27, 29.

14. Franz Oppenheimer, "The Idolatry of the State," *Review of Nations*, no. 2, 1927, p. 26.

15. Franz Oppenheimer, "The Gospel of Freedom," *American Journal of Economics and Sociology*, vol. VII, no. 3, April 1948, p. 353.

16. Ibid., p. 367.

17. See the useful though incomplete two-part bibliography prepared by Felicia Fuss which appeared in the *American Journal of Economics and Sociology*, vol. VI, no. 1, Oct. 1946, pp. 95–112, and vol. VII, no. 1, Oct. 1947, pp. 107–117.

18. Eduard Heimann in *American Journal of Sociology*, vol. XLIX, no. 3, Nov. 1943, p. 225.

19. See Robert M. MacIver and Charles H. Page, *Society* (New York: Holt, Rinehart & Winston, 1961), p. 591, and Robert M. MacIver, *The Modern State* (London: Oxford University Press, 1926), pp. 83–91.

20. E. Adamson Hoebel, *Man in the Primitive World* (New York: McGraw-Hill, 1949), p. 376.

21. Gabriel A. Almond and James S. Coleman, eds., *The Politics of Developing Areas* (Princeton: Princeton University Press, 1960), p. 12.

22. *The State*, p. 14.

23. For some interesting discussion and history of the distinction between society and State, see Randall Collins, "A Comparative Approach to Political Sociology," Reinhard Bendix et al., eds., *State and Society* (Berkeley: University of California Press, 1968), pp. 48–56, and W. G. Runciman, *Social Science and Political Theory* (London: Cambridge University Press, 1969), pp. 24–42.

24. For a brilliant, if sour, look at the decline of social power and the rise of State power in America, see Albert Jay Nock, *Our Enemy, the State* (New York: Free Life Editions, 1974; San Francisco: Fox & Wilkes, 1992).

25. Stanley Diamond, *In Search of the Primitive* (New Brunswick: Transaction Books, 1974), p. 276.

26. Randall Collins, "A Comparative Approach to Political Sociology," op. cit., p. 49.

27. Reinhard Bendix, "Social Stratification and the Political Community," Peter Laslett and W. G. Runciman, eds., *Philosophy, Politics and Society*, Second Series (Oxford: Basil Blackwell, 1969), pp. 224–225.

28. Stanley Diamond, op. cit., p. 9. Also see *The State*, p. 32, and Morris Ginsberg, *Essays in Sociology and Social Philosophy*, vol. I (London: Heinemann, 1956–61), p. 131 ff.

29. For a fascinating view of some of the ways that free and voluntary actions creep into the interstices of our rigid and hierarchical society see Colin Ward, *Anarchy in Action* (New York: Harper & Row, 1974), and Richard Sennett, *The Uses of Disorder* (New York: Alfred A. Knopf, 1970).

30. Edward B. Tylor, *Anthropology: An Introduction to the Study of Man* (London: Watts, 1946), p. 134.

31. Aidan Southall, "A Critique of the Typology of States and Political Systems," Michael Banton, ed., *Political Systems and the Distribution of Power* (London: Tavistock Publications, 1965), p. 121.

32. See M. Fortes and E. E. Evans-Pritchards, eds., *African Political Systems* (London: Oxford University Press, 1940), John Middleton and David Tait, eds., *Tribes Without Rulers* (London: Routledge, 1958), and Aidan Southall, "Stateless Society," *The International Encyclopedia of the Social Sciences*, vol. 15 (New York: Macmillan, 1968).

33. Aidan Southall, "Stateless Society," op. cit., p. 161.

34. F. M. Watkins, *The State as a Concept of Political Science* (New York: Harper & Brothers, 1934), p. 155.

35. Aidan Southall, "Stateless Society," op. cit., p. 167.

36. Lawrence Krader, *Formation of the State* (Englewood Cliffs: Prentice-Hall, 1968), p. 110.

37. Aidan Southall, "Stateless Society," op. cit., p. 167.

38. Joseph R. Strayer, *On the Medieval Origins of the Modern State* (Princeton: Princeton University Press, 1970), p. 13. Also see *The State*, p. 128.

39. Joseph Peden, "Stateless Societies: Ancient Ireland," *The Libertarian Forum*, April 1971, p. 3ff.

40. Murray N. Rothbard, "Individualist Anarchism in the United States: The Origins," *Libertarian Analysis*, Winter 1970, pp. 14–28.

41. See R. H. Lowie, *The Origin of the State* (New York: Russell, 1961), and R. M. MacIver, *The Modern State*, op. cit.

42. Karl A. Wittfogel, *Oriental Despotism* (New Haven: Yale University Press, 1957).

43. Jacques Gernet, *Ancient China, from the Beginnings to the Empire* (London: Faber & Faber, 1968), p. 92.

44. It is relevant to mention here that when Oppenheimer died he was working on a manuscript about the similarities in the development of Japan and Western Europe along lines consistent with *The State*. Four articles entitled "Japan and Western Europe: A Comparative Presentation of Their Social Histories" were published in the *American Journal of Economics and Sociology*, vol. III, no. 4, July 1944, pp. 539–551; vol. IV, no. 1, Oct. 1944, pp. 53–65; vol. IV, no. 2, Jan. 1945, pp. 239–244; and vol. V, no. 1, Oct. 1945, pp. 111–128.

45. For historical information see Howard Becker and Leon Smelo, "Conflict Theories of the Origin of the State," *The Sociological Review*, vol. XXIII, no. 2, July 1931, pp. 65–79.

46. Robert L. Carneiro, *A Theory of the Origin of the State* (Menlo Park: Institute for Humane Studies, n.d.), p. 6.

47. *The State* pp. 6–17, 39–43.

48. *The State*, p. 9.

49. Lawrence Krader, op. cit., p. 45.

50. Ibid.

51. Morton Fried, *The Evolution of Political Society* (New York: Random House, 1967), pp. 225–226.

52. *The State*, p. 26.

53. Georg Simmel, *Conflict* (Glencoe: Free Press, 1955), p. 93. See Lewis Coser, *The Function of Social Conflict* (New York: Free Press, 1956).

54. See Samuel N. Kramer, *The Sumerians* (University of Chicago Press, Chicago, 1963), pp. 73ff.

55. See, for instance, the effects war had on centralizing American society, Ronald Radosh and Murray Rothbard, eds., *A New History of Leviathan* (New York: E. P. Dutton, 1972), and William E. Leuchtenburg, "The New Deal and the Analogue of War," Braeman et al., eds., *Change and Continuity in Twentieth Century America* (New York: Harper & Row, 1966).

56. *The State*, p. 32.

57. *The State*, p. 37.

58. *The State*, p. 8.

59. R. H. Lowie, "The Origin of the State," *The Freeman*, vol. V, no. 123, July 19, 1922, p. 442.

60. *The State*, p. 43.

61. *The State*, p. 44.

62. Morton Fried, op. cit., p. 26. Also see John Schaar, "Legitimacy in the Modern State," Philip Green and Sanford Levinson, eds., *Power and Community in Political Science* (New York: Random House, 1970).

63. *The State*, p. 115.

64. *The State*, p. 123.

65. Franz Oppenheimer, "Reminiscences of Peter Kropotkin," *The Roman Forum*, vol. 2, no. 9, Dec. 1942, p. 11.

66. Ibid.

67. Ibid., p. 12.

68. C. J. Friedrich, "The Deification of the State," *Review of Politics*, vol. I, no. 1, Jan. 1939, p. 21.
69. *The State*, pp. 124–125.

AUTHOR'S PREFACE

This little book has made its way. In addition to the present translation into English, there are authorized editions in French, Hungarian and Serbian. I am also informed that there are translations published in Japanese, Russian, Hebrew and Yiddish; but these, of course, are pirated. The book has stood the test of criticism, and has been judged both favorably and unfavorably. It has, unquestionably, revived the discussion on the origin and essence of the State.

Several prominent ethnologists, particularly Holsti, the present Minister of Foreign Affairs of the Finnish Free State, have attacked the basic principle formulated and demonstrated in this work, but they have failed, because their definition of the State assumed the very matter that required to be proven. They have brought together a large array of facts in proof of the existence of some forms of *Government* and *Leadership*, even where no classes obtained, and to the substance of these forms they have given the name of "The State." It is not my intention to controvert these facts. It is self-evident that in any group of human beings, be it ever so small, there must exist an authority which determines conflicts and, in extraordinary situations, assumes the leadership. But this authority is not "The State," in the sense in which I use the word. The State may be defined as an organization of *one class* dominating over the other classes. Such a class organization can come about in one way only, namely, through conquest and the subjection of ethnic groups by the dominating group. This can be demonstrated with almost mathematical certainty. Not one of my critics has brought proofs to invalidate this thesis. Most modern sociologists, among whom may be named Albion Small, Alfred Vierkandt and Wilhelm Wundt, accept this thesis. Wilhelm Wundt, in particular, asserts in unmistakable language, that "the political society (a term identical with the State in the sense employed in this book) first came about and could originate only in the period of migration and conquest," whereby the subjugation of one people by another was effected.

But even some of my opponents are favorably inclined to my arguments, as in the case of the venerable Adolf Wagner, whose words I am proud to quote. In his article on "The State" in the *Handwörterbuch der Staatswissenschaften*, he writes: "The sociologic concept of the State, to which I have referred, particularly in the broad scope and treatment of it given by Oppenheimer, deserves careful consideration, especially from political economists and political historians. The vista opened out, from this point of view, of the economic development of peoples and that of the State during historic times, should be attractive even to the opponents of the concept itself."

The "sociologic concept of the State," as Ludwig Gumplowicz termed it, is assured of ultimate general acceptance. Its opponents are strenuous and persevering, and I once called them "the sociologic root of all evil"; but the concept, none the less, is the basic principle of "bourgeois" sociology, and will be found of value in the study, not only of economics and history, but in that of Law and Constitutional History. I permit myself to make a few remarks on this point.

The earliest evidence of the recognition of the idea underlying the *law of previous accumulation*, may be traced back, at the latest, to the period of the decay of classical civilization, at the time when the capitalistic slave economy brought the city States to ruin as though their peoples had suffered from a galloping consumption. As in our modern capitalistic age, which resembles that period in many respects, there occurred a breach in all those naturally developed relations in which the individual has found protection. What Ferdinand Toennies calls the "community bonds" were loosened. The individual found himself unprotected, compelled to rely on his own efforts and on his own reason in the seething sea of competition which followed. The collective reason, the product of the wisdom of thousands of years of experience, could no longer guide or safeguard him. It had become scattered. Out of this need for an individual reason, there arose the idea of *nationalism*. This idea had its justification at first, as a line of development and a method in the newly born science of social government; but when later it became what Rubenstein (in his work *Romantic Socialism*) calls a "tendency," it was not justified. The community, to use Toennies' term, changed into a "society." "Contract" seemed to be the only bond that held men

together—the contract based on the purely rationalistic relation of
service for service, the *do ut des*, the "Contrat Social" of Rousseau. A
"society" would thus appear to be a union of self-seeking individuals
who hoped through combination to obtain their personal satisfactions.
Aristotle had taught that the State had developed, by gradual growth,
from the family group. The Stoics and Epicureans held that individuals
formed the State—with this difference, that the former viewed the
individual as being socially inclined by nature, and the latter that he was
naturally anti-social. To the Stoics, therefore, the "State of Nature" was
a peaceful union; to the Epicureans it was a war of each against the other,
with Society as a compelling means for a decent modus vivendi. With
the one a Society was conditioned "physei" (by nature); with the other
it was "nomo" (by decree).

In spite, however, of this fundamental difference between these
schools, both assumed the premise that, at the beginning, individuals
were *free, equal* politically and economically, and that it was from such
an original social order there had developed, through gradual differentiation, the fully developed State with its class hierarchy. This is the *law
of previous accumulation*.

But we should err if we believed that this thesis was originally
intended as a historical account. Rationalism is essentially unhistoric,
even anti-historic. On the contrary, the thesis was originally put forward
as a "fiction," a theory, a conscious unhistorical assumption. In this form
it acquired the name of *natural law*. It was under this name that it came
into modern thought, tinctured stoically in Grotius and Puffendorf, and
epicureanally in Hobbes. It became the operative weapon of thought
among the rising Third Estate of the capitalists.

The capitalists used the weapon, first against the feudal State with its
privileged class, and, later against the Fourth Estate, with its class theory
of Socialism. Against the feudal domination it argued that a "Law of
Nature" knows and permits no privileges. After its victories in the
English Revolution of 1648, and the great French Revolution of 1789,
it justified, by the same reasoning, its own *de facto* pre-eminence, its own
social and economic class superiority, against the claims of the working
classes. According to Adam Smith, the classes in a society are the results
of "natural" development. From an original state of equality, these arose
from no other cause than the exercise of the economic virtues of
industry, frugality and providence. Since these virtues are pre-eminently

those of a bourgeois society, the capitalist rule, thus sanctioned by natural law, is just and unassailable. As a corollary to this theorem the claims of Socialism can not be admitted.

Thus, what originally was put forward as a "fiction," became first, a hypothesis and finally the *axiom* of all bourgeois sociology. Those who support it accept the axiom as self-evident, as not requiring proof. For them, class domination, on this theory, is the result of a gradual differentiation from an original state of general equality and freedom, with no implication in it of any extra-economic power. Robert Malthus applied this alleged law to the future, in his attempt to demonstrate any kind of Socialism to be purely Utopian. His celebrated *Law of Population* is nothing but the *law of original accumulation* projected into the future. He claims that if any attempt were made to restore the state of economic equality, the workings of the law would have the effect—because of the difference in economic efficiency—of restoring modern class conditions. All orthodox sociology begins with the struggle against this supposed law of class formations. Yet every step of progress made in the various fields of the science of sociology, has been made by tearing up, one by one, the innumerable and far-spreading roots which have proceeded from this supposed axiom. A sound sociology has to recall the fact that class formation in historic times did not take place through gradual differentiation in pacific economic competition, but was the result of violent conquest and subjugation.

As both Capitalism and Socialism had their origins in England, these new ideas were certain to find their first expression in that country. So that we find Gerrard Winstanley, the leader of the "true levellers" of Cromwell's time, arraying the facts of history against this anti-historical, theoretical, assumption. He showed that the English ruling class (the Squirearchy) was composed essentially of the victorious conquerors, the Normans, and that the subject class were the conquered English Saxons. But his demonstration had little influence. It was only when the great French Revolution brought the contrast out sharply that the thought sunk in. No less a person than Count Saint-Simon, acknowledged as the founder of the science of modern sociology, and the no less scientific Socialism, discovered in the dominant class of his country the Frankish and Burgundian conquerors, and in its subject population, the descendants of the Romanized Celts. It was the publication of this discovery that gave birth to Western European sociology. The conclusions drawn from it were carried further by St. Simon's disciple, August Comte, in his *Philosophy of History*, and by the Saint Simonists, Enfantin and Bazard. These thinkers had great influence on the economic development of the next century; but their chief contribution was the elaboration of the sociologic idea of the State.

Among the peoples of Western Europe, the new sociology found a readier acceptance than it did among those of Eastern Europe. The reason for this can easily be seen when it is remembered that in the East the contrast between the "State" and "Society" had not been so definitely realized, as it had been in the West. Even in the West, this contrast was only fully appreciated, as a social fact, in England, France, the Netherlands and Italy, because in these countries only the class of mobile wealth which had worked its way up as the Third Estate, had succeeded in ousting the feudal "State." In France, the league of the capitalists with the Crown against the then armed and active nobility had succeeded in subjecting the Frondeurs under the absolute power of the King. From this time on, this new estate represented itself as the Nation, and the term "National Economy" takes the place of the older term "Political Economy." The members of this Third Estate felt themselves to be those subjects of the State whose rights and liberties had been curtailed by the privileges of the two dominant estates of the nobility and the clergy. Henceforth, the Third Estate proclaims the rights of "Society" and against the "State," opposes the eternal Law of Nature—that of original equality and freedom—against the theoretic-historical rights of the Estates. The concept of Society as a contrast to the concept of the State first appears in Locke, and from his time on this contrast was more and more defined, especially in the writings of the physiocrat school of economists.

In this struggle between classes and ideas, neither Middle nor Eastern Europe played any important part. In Germany there had once developed a Capitalist class (in the period of the Fuggers of Augsburg) which attained to almost American magnitude. But it was crushed by the Religious Wars and the various French invasions of the sixteenth and seventeenth centuries, which left Germany a devastated, depopulated desert. At the end of the period there remained a few cities and small states under the absolute domination of princes. Within the cities the artisans were bound together in their craft-leagues, and the rest consisted of those of educational pursuits and academic officials. In a large degree all these were dependent on the State—the members of the craft-guilds because they accepted a privileged condition, the officials because they were servants of the State, and the professional men, because they belonged to the upper estate of the society. For this reason there was no economic or social movement of the Third Estate in Germany; there was only a literary movement influenced by the flow of ideas from the West. This explains why the contrast between the two ideas of the State and of Society was not present in the minds of the German people. On the contrary, the two terms were used as synonyms, both connoting an essentially necessary conformity to nature.

But there is still another cause for this difference in the mental attitude between Western and Eastern Europe. In England and France, from the time of Descartes, the problems and inquiries of science were set by men trained in mathematics and the natural sciences. Especially in the new study of the philosophy of history, the beginning of our modern sociology, did these men act as guides. In Germany, on the contrary, it was the theologians and especially the Protestant theologians who were the leaders of thought. In their hands the State came to be looked upon as an instrument of Divine fashioning, and, indeed, of immanent divinity. This thought resulted in a worship of the State, which reached its height in the well-known Hegelian system. It thus happened that two rivers of thought flowed for a time side by side—the Sociology of Western Europe, and the philosophy of History of Germany—with occasional intercommunicating streams, such as Althusios and Puffendorf into the French, English and Dutch teaching of natural law, and that of Rousseau into Hegel. In 1840, however, a direct junction was effected through Lorenz Stein, one of Hegel's most gifted pupils who, later, became the leading German teacher of administrative law, and influenced generations of thinkers. He came to Paris, as a young man, for the purpose of studying Socialism at the fountain head. He became acquainted with the celebrated men of that heroic time—with Enfantin and Bazard, with Louis Blanc, Reybaud, and Proudhon.

Lorenz Stein absorbed the new thought with enthusiasm, and in his fertile mind there was precipitated the creative synthesis between the Western Europe scientific sociological thought and the metaphysical German philosophy of history. The product was called by him the Science of Society (*Gesellschaftswissenschaft*). It is from the writings of Stein that almost all the important developments of German sociologic thought received their first impulses. Karl Marx, especially (as Struve has shown), as well as Schaeffle, Othmar Spann and Gumplowicz are largely indebted to him.

It is not my purpose to develop this historical theme. I am concerned only in tracing the development of the sociologic idea of the State. The first effect of this meeting of the two streams of thought was a mischievous confusion of terminology. The writers in Western Europe had long ago lost control of the unification of expressions in thinking. As stated above, the Third Estate began by thinking itself to be "Society," as opposed to the State. But when the Fourth Estate grew to class consciousness and became aware of its own theoretic existence, it arrogated to itself the term "Society" (as may be seen from the selection of the word Socialism), and it treated the Bourgeoisie as a form of the "State," of the class State. There were thus two widely differing concepts of "Society." Yet here was an underlying idea common to both Bourgeois and Socialist, since they conceived the State as a collection of privileges arising and maintained *in violation* of natural law, while Society was thought of as the prescribed form of human union in *conformity* with natural law. They differed in one essential only, namely, that while the Third Estate declared its capitalistic Society to be the result of the processes of natural law, the Socialists regarded their aims as not yet attained, and proclaimed that the ideal society of the future, which would really be the product of the processes of natural law, could only be realized by the elimination of all "surplus value." Though both were in conflict with regard to fundamentals, both agreed in viewing the "State" as *civitas diaboli* and "Society" as *civitas dei*.

Stein, however, reversed the objectives of the two concepts. As an Hegelian, and pre-eminently a worshipper of the State, he conceived the State as *civitas coelestis*. Society, which he understood to mean only the dominant bourgeois Society, he viewed through the eyes of his Socialist friends and teachers, and conceived it as *civitas terrena*.

What in Plato's sense is the "pure idea," the "ordre naturel" of the early physiocrats and termed by Frenchmen and Englishmen "Society," was to Stein, the "State." What had been contaminated and made impure by the admixture of coarse matter, they termed the "State," while the German called it "Society." In reality, however, there is little difference between the two. Stein realized with pain that Hegel's pure concept of a State based on right and freedom, was bound to remain an "idea" only.

Eternally fettered, as he assumed it must be, by the forces of property and the culture proceeding from them, it could never be a fact. This is his conclusion regarding "Society," so that its effective development is obstructed by the beneficent association of human beings, as Stein conceived that association.

Thus was attained the very pinnacle of confused thinking. All German sociologists, with the single exception of Carl Dietzel, soon realized that the Hegelian concept of the State was impotent, existing only in the "Idea." In no point did it touch the reality of historical growth, and in no sense could it be made to stand for what had always been considered as the State. Long ago both Marx and Bakunin—respectively the founders of scientific collectivism and practical anarchism—and especially Ludwig Gumplowicz, abandoned the Hegelian terminology and accepted that of Western Europe and this has been generally accepted everywhere.

In this little book I have followed the Western European terminology. By the "State," I do not mean the human aggregation which may perchance *come about to be*, or, as it properly *should be*. I mean by it that summation of privileges and dominating positions which are brought into being by extra-economic power. And in contrast to this, I mean by Society, the totality of concepts of all purely natural relations and institutions between man and man, which will not be fully realized until the last remnant of the creations of the barbaric "ages of conquest and migration," has been eliminated from community life. Others may call any form of leadership and government or some other ideal, the "State." That is a matter of personal choice. It is useless to quarrel about definitions. But it might be well if those other thinkers were to understand that they have not controverted the sociologic idea of the "State," if a concept of the "State" grounded on a different basis, does not correspond to that which they have evolved. And they must guard themselves particularly against the danger of applying any definition other than that used in this book to those actual historical products which have hitherto been called "States," the essence, development, course and future of which must be explained by any true teaching or philosophy of the State.

Franz Oppenheimer
Frankfort-on-Main
April 1922.

THE STATE

I: THEORIES OF THE STATE

This treatise regards the State from the sociological standpoint only, not from the juristic—sociology, as I understand the word, being both a philosophy of history and a theory of economics. Our object is to trace the development of the State from its socio-psychological genesis up to its modern constitutional form; after that we shall endeavor to present a well-founded prognosis concerning its future development. Since we shall trace only the State's inner, essential being, we need not concern ourselves with the external forms of law under which its international and intra-national life is assumed. This treatise, in short, is a contribution to the philosophy of State development; but only in so far as the law of development here traced from its generic form affects also the social problems common to all forms of the modern State.

With this limitation of treatment in mind, we may at the outset dismiss all received doctrines of public law. Even a cursory examination of conventional theories of the State is sufficient to show that they furnish no explanation of its genesis, essence and purpose. These theories represent all possible shadings between all imaginable extremes. Rousseau derives the State from a social contract, while Carey ascribes its origin to a band of robbers. Plato and the followers of Karl Marx endow the State with omnipotence, making it the absolute lord over the citizen in all political and economic matters; while Plato even goes so far as to wish the State to regulate sexual relations. The Manchester school, on the other hand, going to the opposite extreme of liberalism, would have the State exercise only needful police functions, and would thus logically have as a result a scientific anarchism which must utterly exterminate the State. From these various and conflicting views, it is impossible either to establish a fixed principle, or to formulate a satisfactory concept of the real essence of the State.

This irreconcilable conflict of theories is easily explained by the fact that none of the conventional theories treats the State from the sociological view-point. Nevertheless, the State is a phenomenon common to all history, and its essential nature can only be made plain by a broad and comprehensive study of universal history. Except in the field of sociology, the king's highway of science, no treatment of the State has heretofore taken this path. All previous theories of the State have been class theories. To anticipate somewhat the outcome of our researches, every State has been and is a class State, and every theory of the State has been and is a class theory.

A class theory is, however, of necessity, not the result of investigation and reason, but a by-product of desires and will. Its arguments are used, not to establish truth, but as weapons in the contest for material interests. The result, therefore, is not science, but nescience. By understanding the State, we may indeed recognize the essence of theories concerning the State. But the converse is not true. An understanding of theories about the State will give us no clue to its essence.

The following may be stated as a ruling concept, especially prevalent in university teaching, of the origin and essence of the State. It represents a view which, in spite of manifold attacks, is still affirmed.

It is maintained that the State is an organization of human community life, which originates by reason of a social instinct implanted in men by nature (Stoic Doctrine); or else is brought about by an irresistible impulse to end the "war of all against all," and to coerce the savage, who opposes organized effort, to a peaceable community life in place of the anti-social struggle in which all budding shoots of advancement are destroyed (Epicurean Doctrine). These two apparently irreconcilable concepts were fused by the intermediation of mediaeval philosophy. This, founded on theologic reasoning and belief in the Bible, developed the opinion that man, originally and by nature a social creature, is, through original sin, the fratricide of Cain and the transgression at the tower of Babel, divided into innumerable tribes, which fight to the hilt, until they unite peaceably as a State.

This view is utterly untenable. It confuses the logical concept of a class with some subordinate species thereof. Granted that the State is *one* form of organized political cohesion, it is also to be remembered that it is a form having *specific* characteristics. Every State in history was or is a *State of classes*, a polity of superior and inferior social groups, based upon distinctions either of rank or of property. This phenomenon must, then, be called the "State." With it alone history occupies itself.

We should, therefore, be justified in designating every other form of political organization by the same term, without further differentiation, had there never existed any other than a class State, or were it the only conceivable form. At least, proof might properly be called for, to show that each conceivable political organization, even though originally it did not represent a polity of superior and inferior social and economic classes, since it is of necessity subject to inherent laws of development, must in the end be resolved into the specific class form of history. Were such proof forthcoming, it would offer in fact only one form of political amalgamation, calling in turn for differentiation at various stages of development, viz., the preparatory stage, when class distinction does not exist, and the stage of maturity, when it is fully developed.

Former students of the philosophy of the State were dimly aware of this problem. And they tried to adduce the required proof, that because of inherent tendencies of development, every human political organization must gradually become a class State. Philosophers of the canon law handed this theory down to philosophers of the law of nature. From these, through the mediation of Rousseau, it became a part of the teachings of the economists; and even to this day it rules their views and diverts them from the facts.

This assumed proof is based upon the concept of a "primitive accumulation," or an original store of wealth, in lands and in movable property, brought about by means of purely economic forces; a doctrine justly derided by Karl Marx as a "fairy tale." Its scheme of reasoning approximates this:

Somewhere, in some far-stretching, fertile country, a number of free men, of equal status, form a union for mutual protection. Gradually they differentiate into property classes. Those best endowed with strength, wisdom, capacity for saving, industry and caution, slowly acquire a basic amount of real or movable property; while the stupid and less efficient, and those given to carelessness and waste, remain without possessions. The well-to-do lend their productive property to the less well-off in return for tribute, either ground-rent or profit, and become thereby continually richer, while the others always remain poor. These differences in possession gradually develop social class distinctions; since everywhere the rich have preference, while they alone have the time and the means to devote to public affairs and to turn the laws administered by them to their own advantage Thus, in time, there develops a ruling and property-owning estate, and a proletariat, a class without property. The primitive state of free and equal fellows becomes a class State, by an inherent law of development, because in every conceivable mass of men there are, as may readily be seen, strong and weak, clever and foolish, cautious and wasteful ones.

This seems quite plausible, and it coincides with the experience of our daily life. It is not at all unusual to see an especially gifted member of the lower class rise from his former surroundings, and even attain a leading position in the upper class; or conversely, to see some spendthrift or weaker member of the higher group "lose his class" and drop into the proletariat.

And yet this entire theory is utterly mistaken; it is a "fairy tale," or it is a class theory used to justify the privileges of the upper classes. The class State never originated in this fashion, and never could have so originated. History shows that it did not; and economics shows deductively, with a testimony absolute, mathematical and binding, that it could not. A simple problem in elementary arithmetic shows that the assumption of an original accumulation is totally erroneous, and has nothing to do with the development of the class State.

The proof is as follows: All teachers of natural law, etc., have unanimously declared that the differentiation into income-receiving classes and propertyless classes can only take place when all fertile lands have been occupied. For so long as man has ample opportunity to take up unoccupied land, "no one," says Turgot, "would think of entering the service of another"; we may add, "at least for wages, which are not apt to be higher than the earnings of an independent peasant working an unmortgaged and sufficiently large property"; while mortgaging is not possible as long as land is yet free for the working or taking, as free as air and water. Matter that is obtainable for the taking has no value that enables it to be pledged, since no one loans on things that can be had for nothing.

The philosophers of natural law, then, assumed that complete occupancy of the ground must have occurred quite early, because of the natural increase of an originally small population. They were under the impression that at their time, in the eighteenth century, it had taken place many centuries previous, and they naively deduced the existing class aggroupment from the assumed conditions of that long-past point of time. It never entered their heads to work out their problem; and with few exceptions their error has been copied by sociologists, histo-rians and economists. It is only quite recently that my figures were worked out, and they are truly astounding.[*]

We can determine with approximate accuracy the amount of land of average fertility in the temperate zone, and also what amount is sufficient to enable a family of peasants to exist comfortably, or how much such a family can work with its own forces, without engaging outside help or permanent farm servants. At the time of the migration of the barbarians (350 to 750 A.D.), the lot of each able-bodied man was about thirty morgen (equal to twenty acres) on average lands, on very good ground only ten to fifteen morgen (equal to seven or ten acres), four morgen being equal to one hectare. Of this land, at least a third, and sometimes a half, was left uncultivated each year. The remainder of the fifteen to twenty morgen sufficed to feed and fatten into giants the immense families of these child-producing Germans, and this in spite of the primitive technique, whereby at least half the productive capacity of a day was lost. Let us assume that, in these modern times, thirty morgen (equal to twenty acres) for the average peasant suffices to support a family. We have then assumed a block of land sufficiently large to meet any objection. Modern Germany, populated as it is, contains an agricul-tural area of thirty-four million hectares (equal to eighty-four million, fifteen thousand, four hundred and eighty acres). The agricultural population, including farm laborers and their families, amounts to seventeen million; so that, assuming five persons to a family and an equal division of the farm lands, each family would have ten hectares (equal to twenty-five acres). In other words, not even in the Germany of our own day would the point have been reached where, according to the theories of the adherents of natural law, differentiation into classes would begin.

Apply the same process to countries less densely settled, such, for example, as the Danube States, Turkey, Hungary and Russia, and still more astounding results will appear. As a matter of fact, there are still on the earth's surface, seventy-three billion, two hundred million

---

[*] Franz Oppenheimer, *Theorie der Reinen und Politischen Oekonomie*. Berlin, 1912.—*Translator.*

hectares (equal to one hundred eighty billion, eight hundred eighty million and four hundred sixteen thousand acres); dividing into the first amount the number of human beings of all professions whatever, viz., one billion, eight hundred million, every family of five persons could possess about thirty morgen (equal to eighteen and a half acres), *and still leave about two-thirds of the planet unoccupied.*

If, therefore, purely economic causes are ever to bring about a differentiation into classes by the growth of a propertyless laboring class, the time has not yet arrived; and the critical point at which ownership of land will cause a natural scarcity is thrust into the dim future—if indeed it ever can arrive.

As a matter of fact, however, for centuries past, in all parts of the world, we have had a class State, with possessing classes on top and a propertyless laboring class at the bottom, even when population was much less dense than it is to-day. Now it is true that the class State can arise only where all fertile acreage has been *occupied* completely; and since I have shown that even at the present time, all the ground is not occupied economically, this must mean that it has been preempted politically. Since land could not have acquired "natural scarcity," the scarcity must have been "legal." This means that the land has been preempted by a ruling class against its subject class, and settlement prevented. Therefore the State, as a class State, can have originated in no other way than through conquest and subjugation.

This view, the so-called "sociologic idea of the State," as the following will show, is supported in ample manner by well-known historical facts. And yet most modern historians have rejected it, holding that both groups, amalgamated by war into one State, before that time had, each for itself formed a "State." As there is no method of obtaining historical proof to the contrary, since the beginnings of human history are unknown, we should arrive at a verdict of "not proven," were it not that, deductively, there is the absolute certainty that the State, as history shows it, the class State, could not have come about except through warlike subjugation. The mass of evidence shows that our simple calculation excludes any other result.

THE SOCIOLOGICAL IDEA OF THE STATE

To the originally, purely sociological, idea of the State, I have added the economic phase and formulated it as follows:

What, then, is the State as a sociological concept? The State, completely in its genesis, essentially and almost completely during the first stages of its existence, is a social institution, forced by a victorious group of men on a defeated group, with the sole purpose of regulating the dominion of the victorious group over the vanquished, and securing itself against revolt from within and attacks from abroad. Teleologically, this dominion had no other purpose than the economic exploitation of the vanquished by the victors.

No primitive State known to history originated in any other manner.[1] Wherever a reliable tradition reports otherwise, either it concerns the amalgamation of two fully developed primitive States into one body of more complete organization; or else it is an adaptation to men of the fable of the sheep which made a bear their king in order to be protected against the wolf. But even in this latter case, the form and content of the State became precisely the same as in those States where nothing intervened, and which became immediately "wolf States."

The little history learned in our school days suffices to prove this generic doctrine. Everywhere we find some warlike tribe of wild men breaking through the boundaries of some less warlike people, settling down as nobility and founding its State. In Mesopotamia, wave follows wave, State follows State—Babylonians, Amoritans, Assyrians, Arabs, Medes, Persians, Macedonians, Pathians, Mongols, Seldshuks, Tartars, Turks; on the Nile, Hyksos, Nubians, Persians, Greeks, Romans, Arabs, Turks; in Greece, the Doric States are typical examples; in Italy, Romans, Ostrogoths, Lombards, Franks, Germans; in Spain, Carthaginians, Visigoths, Arabs; in Gaul, Romans, Franks, Burgundians, Normans; in Britain, Saxons, Normans. In India wave upon wave of warlike clans has flooded over the country even to the islands of the Indian Ocean. So also is it with China. In the European colonies, we find the selfsame type, wherever a settled element of the population has been found, as for example, in South American and Mexico. Where that element is lacking, where only roving huntsmen are found, who may be exterminated but not subjugated, the conquerors resort to the device of importing from afar masses of men to be exploited, to be subject perpetually to forced labor, and thus the slave trade arises.

An apparent exception is found only in those European colonies in which it is forbidden to replace the lack of a domiciled indigenous population by the importation of slaves. One of these colonies, the United States of America, is among the most powerful State-formations in all history. The exception there found is to be explained by this, that the mass of men to be exploited and worked without cessation *imports itself*, by emigration in great hordes from primitive States or from those in higher stages of development in which exploitation has become unbearable, while liberty of movement has been attained. In this case, one may speak of an infection from afar with "Statehood" brought in by the infected of foreign lands. Where, however, in such colonies, immigration is very limited, either because of excessive distances and the consequent high charges for moving from home, or because of regulations limiting the immigration, we perceive an approximation to the final end of the development of the State, which we nowadays recognize as the necessary outcome and finale, but for which we have not yet found a scientific terminology. Here again, in the dialectic development, a change in the quantity is bound up with a change of the quality. The old form is filled with new contents. We still find a "State" in so far as it represents the tense regulation, secured by external force, whereby is secured the social living together of large bodies of men; but it is no longer the "State" in its older sense. It is no longer the instrument of political domination and economic exploitation of one social group by another; it is no longer a "State of Classes." It rather resembles a condition which appears to have come about through a "social contract." This stage is approached by the Australian Colonies, excepting Queensland, which after the feudal manner still exploits the half enslaved Kanakas. It is almost attained in New Zealand.

So long as there is no general assent as to the origin and essence of States historically known or as to the sociological meaning of the word "State," it would be futile to attempt to force into use a new name for these most advanced commonwealths. They will continue to be called "States" in spite of all protests, especially because of the pleasure of using confusing concepts. For the purpose of this study, however, we propose to employ a new concept, a different verbal lever, and shall speak of the result of the new process as a "Freemen's Citizenship."

This summary survey of the States of the past and present should, if space permitted, be supplemented by an examination of the facts offered by the study of races, and of those States which are not treated in our falsely called "Universal History." On this point, the assurance may be accepted that here again our general rule is valid without exception. Everywhere, whether in the Malay Archipelago, or in the "great sociological laboratory of Africa," at all places on this planet where the development of tribes has at all attained a higher form, the State grew from the subjugation of one group of men by another. Its basic justification, its raison d'etre, was and is the economic exploitation of those subjugated.

The summary review thus far made may serve as proof of the basic premise of this sketch. The pathfinder, to whom, before all others, we are indebted for this line of investigation is Professor Ludwig Gumplowicz of Graz, jurist and sociologist, who crowned a brave life by a brave self-chosen death. We can, then, in sharp outlines, follow in the sufferings of humanity the path which the State has pursued in its progress through the ages. This we propose now to trace from the primitive State founded on conquest to the "freemen's citizenship."

II: The Genesis of the State

One single force impels all life; one force developed it, from the single cell, the particle of albumen floating about in the warm ocean of prehistoric time, up to the vertebrates, and then to man. This one force, according to Lippert, is the tendency to provide for life, bifurcated into "hunger and love." With man, however, philosophy also enters into the play of these forces, in order hereafter, together with "hunger and love, to hold together the structure of the world of men." To be sure, this philosophy, this "idea" of Schopenhauer's, is at its source nothing else than a creature of the provision for life called by him "will." It is an organ of orientation in the world, an arm in the struggle for existence. Yet in spite of this, we shall come to know the desire for causation as a self-acting force, and of social facts as cooperators in the sociological process of development. In the beginning of human society, and as it gradually develops, this tendency pushes itself forward in various bizarre ideas called "superstition." These are based on purely logical conclusions from incomplete observations concerning air and water, earth and fire, animals and plants, which seem endowed with a throng of spirits both friendly and malevolent. One may say that in the most recent modern times, at a stage attained only by very few races, there arises also the younger daughter of the desire for causation, namely science, as a logical result of complete observation of facts; science, now required to exterminate widely branched-out superstition, which, with innumerable threads, has rooted itself in the very soul of mankind.

But, however powerfully, especially in the moment of "ecstasy,"[2] superstition may have influenced history, however powerfully, even in ordinary times, it may have cooperated in the development of human communal life, the principal force of development is still to be found in the necessities of life, which force man to acquire for himself and for his family nourishment, clothing and housing. This remains, therefore, the "economic" impulse. A sociological—and that means a socio-psychological—

investigation of the development of history can, therefore, not progress otherwise than by following out the methods by which economic needs have been satisfied in their gradual unfolding, and by taking heed of the influences of the causation impulse at its proper place.

POLITICAL AND ECONOMIC MEANS

There are two fundamentally opposed means whereby man, requiring sustenance, is impelled to obtain the necessary means for satisfying his desires. These are work and robbery, one's own labor and the forcible appropriation of the labor of others. Robbery! Forcible appropriation! These words convey to us ideas of crime and the penitentiary, since we are the contemporaries of a developed civilization, specifically based on the inviolability of property. And this tang is not lost when we are convinced that land and sea robbery is the primitive relation of life, just as the warrior's trade—which also for a long time is only organized mass robbery—constitutes the most respected of occupations. Both because of this, and also on account of the need of having, in the further development of this study, terse, clear, sharply opposing terms for these very important contrasts, I propose in the following discussion to call one's own labor and the equivalent exchange of one's own labor for the labor of others, the "economic means" for the satisfaction of needs, while the unrequited appropriation of the labor of others will be called the "political means."

The idea is not altogether new; philosophers of history have at all times found this contradiction and have tried to formulate it. But no one of these formulae has carried the premise to its complete logical end. At no place is it clearly shown that the contradiction consists only in the *means* by which the *identical purpose*, the acquisition of economic objects of consumption, is to be obtained. Yet this is the critical point of the reasoning. In the case of a thinker of the rank of Karl Marx, one may observe what confusion is brought about when economic purpose and economic means are not strictly differentiated. All those errors, which in the end led Marx's splendid theory so far away from truth, were grounded in the lack of clear differentiation between the means of economic satisfaction of needs and its end. This led him to designate slavery as an "economic category," and force as an "economic force"—half truths which are far more dangerous than total untruths, since their discovery is more difficult, and false conclusions from them are inevitable.

On the other hand, our own sharp differentiation between the two means toward the same end, will help us to avoid any such confusion. This will be our key to an understanding of the development, the essence, and the purpose of the State; and since all universal history heretofore has been only the history of States, to an understanding of universal history as well. All world history, from primitive times up to our own civilization, presents a single phase, a contest namely between the economic and the political means; and it can present only this phase until we have achieved free citizenship.

PEOPLES WITHOUT A STATE: HUNTSMEN AND GRUBBERS

The State is an organization of the political means. No State, therefore, can come into being until the economic means has created a definite number of objects for the satisfaction of needs, which objects may be taken away or appropriated by warlike robbery. For that reason, primitive huntsmen are without a State; and even the more highly developed huntsmen become parts of a State structure only when they find in their neighborhood an evolved economic organization which they can subjugate. But primitive huntsmen live in practical anarchy.

Grosse says concerning primitive huntsmen in general:

"There are no essential differences of fortune among them, and thus a principal source for the origin of differences in station is lacking. Generally, all grown men within the tribe enjoy equal rights. The older men, thanks to their greater experience, have a certain authority; but no one feels himself bound to render them obedience. Where in some cases chiefs are recognized—as with the Botokude, the Central Californians, the Wedda and the Mincopie—their power is extremely limited. The chieftain has no means of enforcing his wishes against the will of the rest. Most tribes of hunters, however, have no chieftain. The entire society of the males still forms a homogeneous undifferentiated mass, in which only those individuals achieve prominence who are believed to possess magical powers."[3]

Here, then, there scarcely exists a spark of "Statehood," even in the sense of ordinary theories of the State, still less in the sense of the correct "sociologic idea of the State."

The social structure of primitive peasants has hardly more resemblance to a State than has the horde of huntsmen. Where the peasant, working the ground with a grub, is living in liberty, there is as yet no "State." The plow is always the mark of a higher economic condition which occurs only in a State; that is to say, in a system of plantation work carried on by subjugated servants.[4] The grubbers live isolated from one another, scattered over the country in separated curtilages, perhaps in villages, split up because of quarrels about district or farm boundaries. In the best cases, they live in feebly organized associations, bound together by oath, attached only loosely by the tie which the conscious-ness of the same descent and speech and the same belief imposes upon them. They unite perhaps once a year in the common celebration of renowned ancestors or of the tribal god. There is no ruling authority over the whole mass; the various chieftains of a village, or possibly of a district, may have more or less influence in their circumscribed spheres, this depending usually upon their personal qualities, and especially upon the magical powers attributed to them. Cunow describes the Peruvian peasants before the incursion of the Incas as follows: "An unregulated living side by side of many independent, mutually warring tribes, who again were split up into more or less autonomous territorial unions, held together by ties of kinship."[5] One may say that all the primitive peasants of the old and new world were of this type.

In such a state of society, it is hardly conceivable that a warlike organization could come about for purposes of attack. It is sufficiently difficult to mobilize the clan, or still more the tribe, for common defense. The peasant is always lacking in mobility. He is as attached to the ground as the plants he cultivates. As a matter of fact, the working of his field makes him "bound to the soil" (*glebae adscriptus*), even though, in the absence of law, he has freedom of movement. What purpose, moreover, would a looting expedition effect in a country, which throughout its extent is occupied only by grubbing peasants? The peasant can carry off from the peasant nothing which he does not already own. In a condition of society marked by superfluity of agricultural land, each individual contributes only a little work to its extensive cultivation. Each occupies as much territory as he needs. More would be superfluous. Its acquisition would be lost labor, even were its owner able to conserve for any length of time the grain products thus secured. Under primitive conditions, however, this spoils rapidly by reason of change of atmosphere, ants, or other agencies. According to Ratzel, the Central African peasant must convert the superfluous portion of his crops into beer as quickly as possible in order not to lose it entirely!

For all these reasons, primitive peasants are totally lacking in that warlike desire to take the offensive which is the distinguishing mark of hunters and herdsmen: war can not better their condition. And this peaceable attitude is strengthened by the fact that the occupation of the peasant does not make him an efficient warrior. It is true his muscles are strong and he has powers of endurance, but he is sluggish of movement and slow to come to a determination, while huntsmen and nomads by their methods of living develop speed of motion and swiftness of action. For this reason, the primitive peasant is usually of a more gentle disposition than they.*

To sum up: within the economic and social conditions of the peasant districts, one finds no differentiation working for the higher forms of integration. There exists neither the impulse nor the possibility for the warlike subjection of neighbors. No "State" can therefore arise; and, as a matter of fact, none ever has arisen from such social conditions. Had there been no impulse from without, from groups of men nourished in a different manner, the primitive grubber would never have discovered the State.

PEOPLES PRECEDING THE STATE: HERDSMEN AND VIKINGS

Herdsmen, on the contrary, even though isolated, have developed a whole series of the elements of Statehood; and in the tribes which have progressed further, they have developed this in its totality, with the

---

* This psychological contradiction, though often expressly stated, is not the absolute rule, Grosse, *Forms of the Family*, says (page 137): "Some historians of civilization place the peasant in opposition to the warlike nomads, claiming that the peasants are peace-loving peoples. In fact one can not state that their economic life leads them to wars, or educates them for it, as can be said of stock raisers. Nevertheless, one finds within the scope of this form of cultivation a mass of the most warlike and cruel peoples to be found anywhere. The wild cannibals of the Bismarck archipelago, the blood-lusting Vitians, the butchers of men of Dahome and Ashanti—they all cultivate the 'peaceable' acres; and if other peasants are not quite as bad, it seems that the kindly disposition of the vast mass appears to be, at least, questionable."

single exception of the last point of identification which completes the State in its modern sense, that is to say, with exception only of the definitive occupation of a circumscribed territory.

One of these elements is an economic one. Even without the intervention of extra-economic force, there may still develop among herdsmen a sufficiently marked differentiation of property and income. Assuming that, at the start, there was complete equality in the number of cattle, yet within a short time, the one man may be richer and the other poorer. An especially clever breeder will see his herd increase rapidly, while an especially careful watchman and bold hunter will preserve his from decimation by beasts of prey. The element of luck also affects the result. One of these herders finds an especially good grazing ground and healthful watering places; the other one loses his entire stock through pestilence, or through a snowfall or a sandstorm.

Distinctions in fortune quickly bring about class distinctions. The herdsman who has lost all must hire himself to the rich man; and sinking thus under the other, become dependent on him. Wherever herdsmen live, from all three parts of the ancient world, we find the same story. Meitzen reports of the Lapps, nomadic in Norway: "Three hundred reindeer sufficed for one family; who owned only a hundred must enter the service of the richer, whose herds ran up to a thousand head."[6] The same writer, speaking of the Central Asiatic Nomads, says: "A family required three hundred head of cattle for comfort; one hundred head is poverty, followed by a life of debt. The servant must cultivate the lands of the lord."[7] Ratzel reports concerning the Hottentots of Africa a form of "commendatio": "The poor man endeavors to hire himself to the rich man, his only object being to obtain cattle."[8] Laveleye, who reports the same circumstances from Ireland, traces the origin and the name of the feudal system (*système féodal*) to the loaning of cattle by the rich to the poor members of the tribe; accordingly, a "fee-od" (owning of cattle) was the first feud whereby so long as the debt existed the magnate bound the small owner to himself as "his man."

We can only hint at the methods whereby, even in peaceable associations of herdsmen, this economic and consequent social differentiation may have been furthered by the connection of the patriarchate with the offices of supreme and sacrificial priesthood if the wise old men used cleverly the superstition of their clan associates. But this differentiation, so long as it is unaffected by the political means, operates within very modest bounds. Cleverness and efficiency are not hereditary with any degree of certainty. The largest herd will be split up if many heirs grow up in one tent, and fortune is tricky. In our own day, the richest man among the Lapps of Sweden, in the shortest possible time, has been reduced to such complete poverty that the government has had to support him. All these causes bring it about that the original condition of economic and social equality is always approximately restored. "The more peaceable, aboriginal, and genuine the nomad is, the smaller are the tangible differences of possession. It is touching to note the pleasure with which an old prince of the Tsaidam Mongols accepts his tribute or gift, consisting of a handful of tobacco, a piece of sugar, and twenty-five kopeks."[9]

This equality is destroyed permanently and in greater degree by the political means. "Where war is carried on and booty acquired, greater differences arise, which find their expression in the ownership of slaves, women, arms and spirited mounts."[10]

The ownership of *slaves*! The nomad is the inventor of slavery, and thereby has created the seedling of the State, the first economic exploitation of man by man.

The huntsman carries on wars and takes captives. But he does not make them slaves; either he kills them, or else he adopts them into the tribe. Slaves would be of no use to him. The booty of the chase can be stowed away even less than grain can be "capitalized." The idea of using a human being as a labor motor could only come about on an economic plane on which a body of wealth has developed, call it capital, which can be increased only with the assistance of dependent labor forces.

This stage is first reached by the herdsmen. The forces of one family, lacking outside assistance, suffice to hold together a herd of very limited size, and to protect it from attacks of beasts of prey or human enemies. Until the political means is brought into play, auxiliary forces are found very sparingly; such as the poorer members of the clan already mentioned, together with runaways from foreign tribes, who are found all over the world as protected dependents in the suite of the greater owners of herds.[11] In some cases, an entire poor clan of herdsmen enters, half freely, into the service of some rich tribe. "Entire peoples take positions corresponding to their relative wealth. Thus the Tungusen, who are very poor, try to live near the settlements of the Tschuktsches, because they find occupation as herdsmen of the reindeer belonging to the

wealthy Tschuktsches; they are paid in reindeer. And the subjection of
the Ural-Samojedes by the Sirjaenes came about through the gradual
occupation of their pasturing grounds."[12]

Excepting, however, the last named case, which is already very
State-like, the few existing labor forces, without capital, are not sufficient
to permit the clan to keep very large herds. Furthermore, methods of
herding themselves compel division. For a pasture may not, as they say
in the Swiss Alps, be "overpushed," that is to say, have too many cattle
on it. The danger of losing the entire stock is reduced by the measure
in which it is distributed over various pastures. For cattle plagues, storms,
etc., can affect only a part; while even the enemy from abroad can not
drive off all at once. For that reason, the Hereros, for example, "find
every well-to-do owner forced to keep, besides the main herd, several
other subsidiary herds. Younger brothers or other near relatives, or in
want of these, tried old servants, watch them."[13]

For that reason, the developed nomad spares his captured enemy; he
can use him as a slave on his pasture. We may note this transition from
killing to enslaving in a customary rite of the Scythians: they offered up
at their places of sacrifice one out of every hundred captured enemies.
Lippert, who reports this, sees in it "the beginning of a limitation, and
the reason thereof is evidently to be found in the value which a captured
enemy has acquired by becoming the servant of a tribal herdsman."[14]

With the introduction of slaves into the tribal economy of the
herdsmen, the State, in its essential elements, is completed, except that
it has not as yet acquired a definitely circumscribed territorial limit. The
State has thus the *form* of dominion, and its economic basis is the
exploitation of human labor. Henceforth, economic differentiation and
the formation of social classes progress rapidly. The herds of the great,
wisely divided and better guarded by numerous armed servants than
those of the simple freemen, as a rule, maintain themselves at their
original number: they also increase faster than those of the freemen, since
they are augmented by the greater share in the booty which the rich
receive, corresponding to the number of warriors (slaves) which these
place in the field.

Likewise, the office of supreme priest creates an ever-widening
cleft which divides the numbers of the clan, all formerly equals; until
finally a genuine nobility, the rich descendants of the rich patriarchs,
is placed in juxtaposition to the ordinary freemen. "The redskins have

also in their progressive organization developed no nobility and no slavery,* and in this their organization distinguishes itself most essentially from those of the old world. Both arise from the development of the patriarchate of stock-raising people."[15]

Thus we find, with all developed tribes of herdsmen, a social separation into three distinct classes: nobility ("head of the house of his fathers" in the biblical phrase), common freemen, and slaves. According to Mommsen, "all Indo-Germanic people have slavery as a jural institution."[16] This applies to the Aryans and the Semites of Asia and Africa as well as to the Hamites. Among all the Fulbe of the Sahara, "society is divided into princes, chieftains, commons, and slaves."[17] And we find the same facts everywhere, as a matter of course, wherever slavery is legally established, as among the Hova[18] and their Polynesian kinsmen, the "Sea Nomads." Human psychology under similar circumstances brings about like conditions, independent of color and race.

Thus the herdsman gradually becomes accustomed to earning his livelihood through warfare, and to the exploitation of men as servile labor motors. And one must admit that his entire mode of life impels him to make more and more use of the "political means."

He is physically stronger and just as adroit and determined as the primitive huntsman, whose food supply is too irregular to permit him to attain his greatest natural physical development. The herdsman can, in all cases, grow to his full stature, since he has uninterrupted nourishment in the milk of his herds and an unfailing supply of meat. This is shown in the Arian horse nomad, no less than in the herdsman of Asia and Africa, e.g., the Zulu. Secondly, tribes of herdsmen increase faster than hordes of hunters. This is so, not only because adults can obtain much more nourishment from a given territory, but still more because possession of the milk of animals shortens the period of nursing for the mothers, and consequently permits a greater number of children to be born and to grow to maturity. As a consequence, the pastures and steppes of the old world became inexhaustible fountains, which periodically

---

* This statement of Lippert is not quite correct. The higher developed domiciled huntsmen and fishermen of Northwest America have both nobles and slaves.

burst their confines letting loose inundations of humanity, so that they came to be called the *"vaginae gentium."*

Moreover we find a much larger number of armed warriors among herdsmen than among hunters. Each of these herdsmen is stronger individually, and yet all of them together are at least as mobile as is a horde of huntsmen; while the camel and horse riders among them are incomparably more mobile. This greater mass of the best individual elements is held together by an organization only possible under the aegis of a slave-holding patriarchate accustomed to rule, an organization prepared and developed by its occupation, and therefore superior to that of the young warriors of the huntsmen sworn to the service of one chief.

Hunters, it may be observed, work best alone or in small groups. Herdsmen, on the other hand, move to the best advantage in a great train, in which each individual is best protected; and which is in every sense an armed expedition, where every stopping place becomes an armed camp. Thus there is developed a science of tactical maneuvers, strict subordination, and firm discipline. "One does not make a mistake," as Ratzel says, "if one accounts as the disciplinary forces in the life of the nomads the order of the tents which, in the same form, exists since most ancient times. Every one and everything here has a definite, traditional place; hence the speed and order in setting up and in breaking camp, in establishment and in rearrangement. It is unheard of that any one without orders, or without the most pressing reason, should change his place. Thanks to this strict discipline, the tents can be packed up and loaded away within the space of an hour."[19]

The same tried order, handed down from untold ages, regulates the warlike march of the tribe of herdsmen while on the hunt, in war and in peaceable wandering. Thus they become professional fighters, irresistible until the State develops higher and mightier organizations. Herdsman and warrior become identical concepts. Ratzel's statement concerning the Central Asiatic Nomads applies to them all: "The nomad is, as herdsman, an economic, as warrior, a political concept. It is easy for him to turn from any activity to that of the warrior and robber. Everything in life has for him a pacific and war-like, an honest and robber-like, side; according to circumstances, the one or the other of these phases appears uppermost. Even fishing and navigation, at the hands of the East Caspian Turkomans, developed into piracy. . . . The activities of the apparently pacific existence as a herdsman determine those of the warrior; the pastoral crook becomes a fighting implement. In the fall, when the horses return strengthened from the pasture and the second cropping of the sheep is completed, the nomads' minds turn to some feud or robbing expedition (*Baranta*, literally, to make cattle, to lift cattle), adjourned to that time. This is an expression of the right of self help, which in contentions over points of law, or in quarrels affecting dignity, or in blood feuds, seeks both requital and surety in the most valuable things that the enemy possesses, namely, the animals of his herd. Young men who have not been on a *baranta* must first acquire the name *batir*, hero, and thus earn the claim to honor and respect. The pleasure of ownership joined to the desire for adventure develops the triple descending gradation of avenger, hero, and robber."[20]

An identical development takes place with the sea nomads, the "Vikings," as with the land nomads. This is quite natural, since in the most important cases noted in the history of mankind, sea nomads are simply land nomads taking to the sea.

We have noted above one of the innumerable examples which indicate that the herdsman does not long hesitate to use for marauding expeditions, instead of the horse or the "ship of the desert," the "horses of the sea." This case is exemplified by the East Caspian Turkomans.[21] Another example is furnished by the Scythians: "From the moment when they learn from their neighbors the art of navigating the seas, these wandering herdsmen, whom Homer (*Iliad*, XIII, 3) calls 'respected horsemen, milk-eaters and poor, the most just of men,' change into daring navigators like their Baltic and Scandinavian brethren. Strabo (*Cas.*, 301) complains: 'Since they have ventured on the sea, carrying on piracy and murdering foreigners, they have become worse; and associating with many peoples, they adopt their petty trading and spendthrift habits.' "[22]

If the Phoenicians really were "Semites," they furnish an additional example of incomparable importance of the transformation of land into "sea Bedouins," i.e., warlike robbers; and the same is probably true for the majority of the numerous peoples who looted the rich countries around the Mediterranean, whether from the coast of Asia Minor, Dalmatia, or from the North African shore. These begin from the earliest times, as we see from the Egyptian monuments (the Greeks were not admitted into Egypt),[23] and continue to the present day: e.g., the Riff pirates. The North African "Moors," an amalgamation of Arabs and of

Berbers, both originally land nomads, are perhaps the most celebrated example of this change.

There are cases in which sea nomads—that is to say, sea robbers—arise immediately from fishermen, with no intermediate herdsman stage. We have already examined the causes which give the herdsmen their superiority over the peasantry: the relatively numerous population of the horde, combined with an activity which develops courage and quick resolution in the individual, and educates the mass as a whole to tense discipline. All this applies also to fishermen dwelling on the sea. Rich fishing grounds permit a considerable density of population, as is shown in the case of the Northwest Indians (Tlinkit, etc.); these permit also the keeping of slaves, since the slave earns more by fishing than his keep amounts to. Thus we find, here alone among the redskins, slavery developed as an institution, and we find, therefore, along with it, permanent economic differences among the freemen, which result in a sort of plutocracy similar to that noted among herdsmen. Here, as there, the habit of command over slaves produces the habit of rule and a taste for the "political means." This is favored by the tense discipline developed in navigation. "Not the least advantage of fishing in common is found in the discipline of the crews. They must render implicit obedience to a leader chosen in each of the larger fishing boats, since every success depends upon obedience The command of a ship afterward facilitates the command of the State. We are accustomed to reckon the Solomon Islanders as complete savages, and yet their life is subject to one solitary element, which combines their forces, namely, navigation."[24] If the Northwest Indians did not become such celebrated sea robbers as their likes in the old world, this is due to the fact that the neighborhoods within their reach had developed no rich civilization; but all the more developed fishermen carry on piracy.

For this reason, the Vikings have the same capacity to choose the political means as the basis of their economic existence as have the cattle raiders; and similarly they have been founders of States on a large scale. Hereafter, we shall distinguish the States founded by them as "sea States," while the States founded by herdsmen—and in the new world by hunters—will be called "land States." Sea States will be treated extensively when we discuss the consequences of the *developed feudal State.* As long, however, as we are discussing the development of the State, and the *primitive* feudal State, we must limit ourselves to the consideration of the land State and leave the sea State out of account. This treatment is convenient, since in all essential things the sea State has the same characteristics, but its development can not be followed through the various typical States as can the development of the land State.

THE GENESIS OF THE STATE

The hordes of huntsmen are incomparably weaker, both in numbers and in the strength of the single fighters, than are the herdsmen with whom they occasionally brush. Naturally they can not withstand the impact. They flee to the highlands and mountains, where the herdsmen have no inclination to follow them, not only because of the physical hardships involved, but also because their cattle do not find pasturage there; or else they enter into a form of cliental relation, as happened often in Africa, especially in very ancient times. When the Hyksos invaded Egypt, such dependent huntsmen followed them. The huntsmen usually pay for protection an inconsiderable tribute in the form of spoils of the chase, and are used for reconnoitering and watching. But the huntsman, being a "practical anarchist," often invites his own destruction rather than submit to regular labor. For these reasons, no "State" ever arose from such contact.

The peasants fight as undisciplined levies, and with their single combatants undisciplined; so that, in the long run, even though they are strong in numbers, they are no more able than are the hunters to withstand the charge of the heavily armed herdsmen. But the peasantry do not flee. The peasant is attached to his ground, and has been used to regular work. He remains, yields to subjection, and pays tribute to his conqueror; *that is the genesis of the land States in the old world.*

In the new world, where the larger herding animals, cattle, horses, camels, were not indigenous, we find that instead of the herdsman the hunter is the conqueror of the peasant, because of his infinitely superior adroitness in the use of arms and in military discipline. "In the old world we found that the contrast of herdsmen and peasants developed civilization; in the new world the contrast is between the sedentary and the roving tribes. The Toltecks, devoted to agriculture, fought wild tribes (with a highly developed military organization) breaking in from the north, as endlessly as did Iran with Turan."[25]

This applies not only to Peru and Mexico, but to all America, a strong ground for the opinion that the fundamental basis of civilization is the same all over the world, its development being consistent and regular under the most varied economic and geographical conditions. Wherever opportunity offers, and man possesses the power, he prefers political to economic means for the preservation of his life. And perhaps this is true not alone of man, for, according to Maeterlinck's *Life of the Bees*, a swarm which has once made the experiment of obtaining honey from a foreign hive, by robbery instead of by tedious building, is thenceforth spoiled for the "economic means." From working bees, robbers bees have developed.

Leaving out of account the State formations of the new world, which have no great significance in universal history, the cause of the genesis of all States is the contrast between peasants and herdsmen, between laborers and robbers, between bottom lands and prairies. Ratzel, regarding sociology from the geographical view-point, expresses this cleverly: "It must be remembered that nomads do not always destroy the opposing civilization of the settled folk. This applies not only to tribes, but also to States, even to those of some might. The war-like character of the nomads is a great factor in the creation of States. It finds expression in the immense nations of Asia controlled by nomad dynasties and nomad armies, such as Persia, ruled by the Turks; China, conquered and governed by the Mongols and Manchus; and in the Mongol and Radjaputa States of India, as well as in the States on the border of the Soudan, where the amalgamation of the formerly hostile elements has not yet developed so far, although they are joined together by mutual benefit. In no place is it shown so clearly as here on the border of the nomad and peasant peoples, that the great workings of the impulse making for civilization on the part of the nomads are not the result of civilizing activity, but of war-like exploits at first detrimental to pacific work. Their importance lies in the capacity of the nomads to hold together the sedentary races who otherwise would easily fall apart. This, however, does not exclude their learning much from their subjects. . . . Yet all these industrious and clever folk did not have and could not have the will and the power to rule, the military spirit, and the sense for the order and subordination that befits a State. For this reason, the desert-born lords of the Soudan rule over their negro folk just as the Manchus rule their Chinese subjects. This takes place pursuant to a law, valid from Timbuctoo to Pekin, whereby advantageous State formations arise in rich peasant lands adjoining a wide prairie; where a high material culture of sedentary peoples is violently subjugated to the service of prairie dwellers having energy, war-like capacity, and desire to rule."[26]

In the genesis of the State, from the subjection of a peasant folk by a tribe of herdsmen or by sea nomads, six stages may be distinguished. In the following discussion it should not be assumed that the actual historical development must, in each particular case, climb the entire scale step by step. Although, even here, the argument does not depend upon bare theoretical construction, since every particular stage is found in numerous examples, both in the world's history and in ethnology, and there are States which have apparently progressed through them all. But there are many more which have skipped one or more of these stages.

The first stage comprises robbery and killing in border fights, endless combats broken neither by peace nor by armistice. It is marked by killing of men, carrying away of children and women, looting of herds, and burning of dwellings. Even if the offenders are defeated at first, they return in stronger and stronger bodies, impelled by the duty of blood feud. Sometimes the peasant group may assemble, may organize its militia, and perhaps temporarily defeat the nimble enemy; but mobilization is too slow and supplies to be brought into the desert too costly for the peasants. The peasants' militia does not, as does the enemy, carry its stock of food—its herds—with it into the field. In Southwest Africa the Germans recently experienced the difficulties which a well-disciplined and superior force, equipped with a supply train, with a railway reaching back to its base of supply, and with millions of the German Empire behind it, may have with a handful of herdsmen warriors, who were able to give the Germans a decided setback. In the case of primitive levies, this difficulty is increased by the narrow spirit of the peasant, who considers only his own neighborhood, and by the fact that while the war is going on the lands are uncultivated. Therefore, in such cases, in the long run, the small but compact and easily mobilized body constantly defeats the greater disjointed mass, as the panther triumphs over the buffalo.

This is the first stage in the formation of States. The State may remain stationary at this point for centuries, for a thousand years. The following is a thoroughly characteristic example:

"Every range of a Turkoman tribe formerly bordered upon a wide belt which might be designated as its 'looting district.' Everything north and east of Chorassan, though nominally under Persian dominion, has for decades belonged more to the Turkomans, Jomudes, Goklenes, and other tribes of the bordering plains, than to the Persians. The Tekinzes, in a similar manner, looted all the stretches from Kiwa to Bokhara, until other Turkoman tribes were successfully rounded up either by force or by corruption to act as a buffer. Numberless further instances can be found in the history of the chain of oases which extends between Eastern and Western Asia directly through the steppes of its central part, where since ancient times the Chinese have exercised a predominant influence through their possession of all important strategic centers, such as the Oasis of Chami. The nomads, breaking through from north and south, constantly tried to land on these islands of fertile ground, which to them must have appeared like Islands of the Blessed. And every horde, whether laden down with booty or fleeing after defeat, was protected by the plains. Although the most immediate threats were averted by the continued weakening of the Mongols, and the actual dominion of Thibet, yet the last insurrection of the Dunganes showed how easily the waves of a mobile tribe break over these islands of civilization. Only after the destruction of the nomads, impossible as long as there are open plains in Central Asia, can their existence be definitely secured."[27]

The entire history of the old world is replete with well-known instances of mass expeditions, which must be assigned to the first stage of State development, inasmuch as they were intent, not upon conquest, but directly on looting. Western Europe suffered through these expeditions at the hands of the Celts, Germans, Huns, Avars, Arabs, Magyars, Tartars, Mongolians and Turks by land; while the Vikings and the Saracens harassed it on the waterways. These hordes inundated entire continents far beyond the limits of their accustomed looting ground. They disappeared, returned, were absorbed, and left behind them only wasted lands. In many cases, however, they advanced in some part of the inundated district directly to the sixth and last stage of State formation, in cases namely, where they established a permanent dominion over the peasant population. Ratzel describes these mass migrations excellently in the following:

"The expeditions of the great hordes of nomads contrast with this movement, drop by drop and step by step, since they overflow with

tremendous power, especially Central Asia and all neighboring countries. The nomads of this district, as of Arabia and Northern Africa, unite
mobility in their way of life with an organization holding together their
entire mass for one single object. It seems to be a characteristic of the
nomads that they easily develop despotic power and far-reaching might
from the patriarchal cohesion of the tribe. Mass governments thereby
come into being, which compare with other movements among men
in the same way that swollen streams compare with the steady but
diffused flow of a tributary. The history of China, India, and Persia, no
less than that of Europe, shows their historical importance. Just as they
moved about on their ranges with their wives and children, slaves and
carts, herds and all their paraphernalia, so they inundated the border-
lands. While this ballast may have deprived them of speed it increased
their momentum. The frightened inhabitants were driven before them,
and like a wave they rolled over the conquered countries, absorbing
their wealth. Since they carried everything with them, their new abodes
were equipped with all their possessions, and thus their final settlements
were of an ethnographic importance. After this manner, the Magyars
flooded Hungary, the Manchus invaded China, the Turks, the countries
from Persia to the Adriatic."[28]

What has been said here of Hamites, Semites and Mongolians, may
be said also, at least in part, of the Aryan tribes of herdsmen. It applies
also to the true negroes, at least to those who live entirely from their
herds: "The mobile, warlike tribes of the Kafirs possess a power of
expansion which needs only an enticing object in order to attain violent
effects and to overturn the ethnologic relations of vast districts. Eastern
Africa offers such an object. Here the climate did not forbid stock raising,
as in the countries of the interior, and did not paralyze from the start,
the power of impact of the nomads, while nevertheless numerous
peaceable agricultural peoples found room for their development.
Wandering tribes of Kafirs poured like devastating streams into the
fruitful lands of the Zambesi, and up to the highlands between the
Tanganyika and the coast. Here they met the advance guard of the
Watusi, a wave of Hamite eruption, coming from the north. The former
inhabitants of these districts were either exterminated, or as serfs cultivated the lands which they formerly owned; or they still continued to
fight; or again, they remained undisturbed in settlements left on one side
by the stream of conquest."[29]

All this has taken place before our eyes. Some of it is still going on. During many thousands of years it has "jarred all Eastern Africa from the Zambesi to the Mediterranean." The incursion of the Hyksos, whereby for over five hundred years Egypt was subject to the shepherd tribes of the eastern and northern deserts—"kinsmen of the peoples who up to the present day herd their stock between the Nile and the Red Sea"[30]—is the first authenticated foundation of a State. These States were followed by many others both in the country of the Nile itself, and farther southward, as far as the Empire of Muata Jamvo on the southern rim of the central Congo district, which Portuguese traders in Angola reported as early as the end of the sixteenth century, and down to the Empire of Uganda, which only in our own day has finally succumbed to the superior military organization of Europe. "Desert land and civilization never lie peaceably alongside one another; but their battles are alike and full of repetitions."[31]

"Alike and full of repetitions"! That may be said of universal history on its basic lines. The human ego in its fundamental aspect is much the same all the world over. It acts uniformly in obedience to the same influences of its environment, with races of all colors, in all parts of the earth, in the tropics as in the temperate zones. One must step back far enough and choose a point of view so high that the variegated aspect of the details does not hide the great movements of the mass. In such a case, our eye misses the "mode" of fighting, wandering, laboring humanity, while its "substance," ever similar, ever new, ever enduring through change, reveals itself under uniform laws.

Gradually, from this first stage, there develops the second, in which the peasant, through thousands of unsuccessful attempts at revolt, has accepted his fate and has ceased every resistance. About this time, it begins to dawn on the consciousness of the wild herdsman that a murdered peasant can no longer plow, and that a fruit tree hacked down will no longer bear. In his own interest, then, wherever it is possible, he lets the peasant live and the tree stand. The expedition of the herdsmen comes just as before, every member bristling with arms, but no longer intending nor expecting war and violent appropriation. The raiders burn and kill only so far as is necessary to enforce a wholesome respect, or to break an isolated resistance. But in general, principally in accordance with a developing customary right—the first germ of the development of all public law—the herdsman now appropriates only the surplus of the peasant. That is to say, he leaves the peasant his house, his gear and his provisions up to the next crop.[*] The herdsman in the first stage is like the bear, who for the purpose of robbing the beehive, destroys it. In the second stage he is like the bee-keeper, who leaves the bees enough honey to carry them through the winter.

Great is the progress between the first stage and the second. Long is the forward step, both economically and politically. In the beginning, as we have seen, the acquisition by the tribe of herdsmen was purely an occupying one. Regardless of consequences, they destroyed the source of future wealth for the enjoyment of the moment. Henceforth the acquisition becomes economical, because all economy is based on wise housekeeping, or in other words, on restraining the enjoyment of the moment in view of the needs of the future. The herdsman has learned to "capitalize." It is a vast step forward in politics when an utterly strange human being, prey heretofore like the wild animals, obtains a value and is recognized as a source of wealth. Although this is the beginning of all slavery, subjugation, and exploitation, it is at the same time the genesis of a higher form of society, that reaches out beyond the family based upon blood relationship. We saw how, between the robbers and the robbed, the first threads of a jural relation were spun across the cleft which separated those who had heretofore been only "mortal enemies." The peasant thus obtains a semblance of *right* to the bare necessaries of life; so that it comes to be regarded as *wrong* to kill an unresisting man or to strip him of everything.

And better than this, gradually more delicate and softer threads are woven into a net very thin as yet, but which, nevertheless, brings about more human relations than the customary arrangement of the division of spoils. Since the herdsmen no longer meet the peasants in combat only, they are likely now to grant a respectful request, or to remedy a well grounded grievance. "The categorical imperative" of equity, "Do

---

[*] Ratzel, l. c. II, page 393, in speaking of the Arabs says: "The difficulty of nourishing slaves makes it impossible to keep them. Vast populations are kept in subjection and deprived of everything beyond the necessaries for maintaining life. They turn entire oases into demesne lands, visited at the harvest time in order to rob the inhabitants; a domination characteristic of the desert."

to others as you would have them do unto you," had heretofore ruled the herdsmen only in their dealings with their own tribesmen and kind. Now for the first time it begins to speak, shyly whispering in behalf of those who are alien to blood relationship. In this, we find the germ of that magnificent process of external amalgamation which, out of small hordes, has formed nations and unions of nations; and which in the future is to give life to the concept of "humanity." We find also the germ of the internal unification of tribes once separated, from which, in place of the hatred of "barbarians," will come the all comprising love of humanity, of Christianity and Buddhism.

The moment when first the conqueror spared his victim in order permanently to exploit him in productive work, was of incomparable historical importance. It gave birth to nation and State, to right and the higher economics, with all the developments and ramifications which have grown and which will hereafter grow out of them. The root of everything human reaches down into the dark soil of the animal—love and art, no less than State, justice and economics.

Still another tendency knots yet more closely these psychic relations. To return to the comparison of the herdsman and the bear, there are in the desert, beside the bear who guards the bees, other bears who also lust after honey. But our tribe of herdsmen blocks their way, and protects its beehives by force of arms. The peasants become accustomed, when danger threatens, to call on the herdsmen, whom they no longer regard as robbers and murderers, but as protectors and saviors. Imagine the joy of the peasants when the returning band of avengers brings back to the village the looted women and children, with the enemies' heads or scalps. These ties are no longer threads, but strong and knotted bands.

Here is one of the principal forces of that "integration," whereby in the further development, those originally not of the same blood, and often enough of different groups speaking different languages, will in the end be welded together into *one* people, with *one* speech, *one* custom, and *one* feeling of nationality. This unity grows by degrees from common suffering and need, common victory and defeat, common rejoicing and common sorrow. A new and vast domain is open when master and slave serve the same interests; then arises a stream of sympathy, a sense of common service. Both sides apprehend, and gradually recognize, each other's common humanity. Gradually the points of similarity are sensed, in place of the differences in build and apparel, of language and religion, which had heretofore brought about only antipathy and hatred. Gradually they learn to understand one another, first through a common speech, and then through a common mental habit. The net of the psychical inter-relations becomes stronger.

In this second stage of the formation of States, the ground work, in its essentials, has been mapped out. No further step can be compared in importance to the transition whereby the bear becomes a bee-keeper. For this reason, short references must suffice.

The third stage arrives when the "surplus" obtained by the peasantry is brought by them regularly to the tents of the herdsmen as "tribute," a regulation which affords to both parties self-evident and considerable advantages. By this means, the peasantry is relieved entirely from the little irregularities connected with the former method of taxation, such as a few men knocked on the head, women violated, or farmhouses burned down. The herdsmen on the other hand, need no longer apply to this "business" any "expense" and labor, to use a mercantile expression; and they devote the time and energy thus set free toward an "extension of the works," in other words, to subjugating other peasants.

This form of tribute is found in many well-known instances in history: Huns, Magyars, Tartars, Turks, have derived their largest income from their European tributes. Sometimes the character of the tribute paid by the subjects to their master is more or less blurred, and the act assumes the guise of payment for protection, or indeed, of a subvention. The tale is well known whereby Attila was pictured by the weakling emperor at Constantinople as a vassal prince; while the tribute he paid to the Hun appeared as a fee.

The fourth stage, once more, is of very great importance, since it adds the decisive factor in the development of the State, as we are accustomed to see it, namely, the union on one strip of land of both ethnic groups.[*]

---

[*] There is apparently in the case of the Fulbe, a transition stage between the first three stages and the fourth, in which dominion is exercised half internationally and half intra-nationally. According to Ratzel (l. c. II, page 419): "Like a cuttle-fish, the conquering race stretches numerous arms hither and thither among the terrified aborigines, whose lack of cohesion affords plenty of gaps. Thus the Fulbe are slowly flowing into the Benue countries and quite gradually permeating them. Later observers have thus quite rightly abstained from assigning definite boundaries. There are many scattered Fulbe

(It is well known that no jural definition of a State can be arrived at without the concept of State territory.) From now on, the relation of the two groups, which was originally international, gradually becomes more and more intra-national.

This territorial union may be caused by foreign influences. It may be that stronger hordes have crowded the herdsmen forward, or that their increase in population has reached the limit set by the nutritive capacity of the steppes or prairies; it may be that a great cattle plague has forced the herdsmen to exchange the unlimited scope of the prairies for the narrows of some river valley. In general, however, internal causes alone suffice to bring it about that the herdsmen stay in the neighborhood of their peasants. The duty of protecting their tributaries against other "bears" forces them to keep a levy of young warriors in the neighborhood of their subjects; and this is at the same time an excellent measure of defense since it prevents the peasants from giving way to a desire to break their bonds, or to let some other herdsmen become their overlords. This latter occurrence is by no means rare, since, if tradition is correct, it is the means whereby the sons of Rurik came to Russia.

As yet the local juxtaposition does not mean a State community in its narrowest sense; that is to say, a unital organization.

In case the herdsmen are dealing with utterly unwarlike subjects, they carry on their nomad life, peaceably wandering up and down and herding their cattle among the perioike and helots. This is the case with the light-colored Wahuma,[32] "the handsomest men of the world" (Kandt), in Central Africa, or the Tuareg clan of the Hadanara of the Asgars, "who have taken up their seats among the Imrad and have become wandering freebooters. These Imrad are the serving class of the Asgars, who live on them, although the Imrad could put into the field ten times as many warriors; the situation is analogous to that of the Spartans in relation to their Helots."[33] The same may be said of the Teda

---

localities which look to a particular place as their center and as the center of their power. Thus Muri is the capital of the numerous Fulbe settlements scattered about the Middle Benue, and the position of Gola is similar in the Adamawa district. As yet there are no proper kingdoms with defined frontiers against each other and against independent tribes. Even these capitals are in other respects still far from being firmly settled."

among the neighboring Borku: "Just as the land is divided into a semi-desert supporting the nomads, and gardens with date groves, so the population is divided between nomads and settled folk. Although about equal in number, ten to twelve thousand altogether, it goes without saying that these latter are subject to the others."[34]

And the same applies to the entire group of herdsmen known as the Galla Masi and Wahuma. "Although differences in possessions are considerable, they have few slaves, as a serving class. These are represented by peoples of a lower caste, who live separate and apart from them. It is herdsmanship which is the basis of the family, of the State, and along with these of the principle of political evolution. In this wide territory, between Scehoa and its southernmost boundaries, on the one hand, and Zanzibar on the other, there is found no strong political power, in spite of the highly developed social articulation."[35]

In case the country is not adapted to herding cattle on a large scale—as was universally the case in Western Europe—or where a less unwarlike population might make attempts at insurrection, the crowd of lords becomes more or less permanently settled, taking either steep places or strategically important points for their camps, castles, or towns. From these centers, they control their "subjects," mainly for the purpose of gathering their tribute, paying no attention to them in other respects. They let them administer their affairs, carry on their religious worship, settle their disputes, and adjust their methods of internal economy. Their autochthonous constitution, their local officials, are, in fact, not interfered with.

If Frants Buhl reports correctly, that was the beginning of the rule of the Israelites in Canaan.[36] Abyssinia, that great military force, though at the first glance it may appear to be a fully developed State, does not, however, seem to have advanced beyond the fourth stage. At least Ratzel states: "The principal care of the Abyssinians consists in the tribute, in which they follow the method of oriental monarchs in olden and modern times, which is not to interfere with the internal management and administration of justice of their subject peoples."[37]

The best example of the fourth stage is found in the situation in ancient Mexico before the Spanish conquest: "The confederation under the leadership of the Mexicans had somewhat more progressive ideas of conquest. Only those tribes were wiped out that offered resistance. In other cases, the vanquished were merely plundered, and then required to pay tribute. The defeated tribe governed itself just as before, through its own officials. It was different in Peru, where the formation of a compact empire followed the first attack. In Mexico, intimidation and exploitation were the only aims of the conquest. And so it came about that the so-called Empire of Mexico at the time of the conquest represented merely a group of intimidated Indian tribes, whose federation with one another was prevented by their fear of plundering expeditions from some unassailable fort in their midst."[38] It will be observed that one can not speak of this as a State in any proper sense. Ratzel shows this in the note following the above: "It is certain that the various points held in subjection by the warriors of Montezuma were separated from one another by stretches of territory not yet conquered. A condition very like the rule of the Hova in Madagascar. One would not say that scattering a few garrisons, or better still, military colonies, over the land, is a mark of absolute dominion, since these colonies, with great trouble, maintain a strip of a few miles in subjection."[39]

The logic of events presses quickly from the fourth to the fifth stage, and fashions almost completely the full State. Quarrels arise between neighboring villages or clans, which the lords no longer permit to be fought out, since by this the capacity of the peasants for service would be impaired. The lords assume the right to arbitrate, and in case of need, to enforce their judgment. In the end, it happens that at each "court" of the village king or chief of the clan there is an official deputy who exercises the power, while the chiefs are permitted to retain the appearance of authority. The State of the Incas shows, in a primitive condition, a typical example of this arrangement.

Here we find the Incas united at Cuzco where they had their patrimonial lands and dwellings.[40] A representative of the Incas, the Tucricuc, however, resided in every district at the court of the native chieftain. He "had supervision over all affairs of his district; he raised the troops, superintended the delivery of the tribute, ordered the forced labor on roads and bridges, superintended the administration of justice, and in short supervised everything in his district."[41]

The same institutions which have been developed by American huntsmen and Semite shepherds are found also among African herdsmen. In Ashanti, the system of the Tucricuc has been developed in a typical fashion;[42] and the Dualla have established for their subjects living in segregated villages "an institution based on conquest midway between a feudal system and slavery."[43] The same author reports that the Barotse have a constitution corresponding to the earliest stage of the mediaeval feudal organization: "Their villages are . . . as a rule surrounded by a circle of hamlets where their serfs live. These till the fields of their lords in the immediate neighborhood, grow grain, or herd the cattle."[44] The only thing that is not typical here consists in this, that the lords do not live in isolated castles or halls, but are settled in villages among their subjects.

It is only a very small step from the Incas to the Dorians in Lacedaemon, Messenia, or Crete; and no greater distance separates the Fulbe, Dualla and Barotse from the comparatively rigidly organized feudal States of the African Negro Empires of Uganda, Unyoro, etc.; and the corresponding feudal empires of Eastern and Western Europe and of all Asia. In all places, the same results are brought about by force of the same socio-psychological causes. The necessity of keeping the subjects in order and at the same time of maintaining them at their full capacity for labor, leads step by step from the fifth to the sixth stage, in which the State, by acquiring full intra-nationality and by the evolution of "Nationality," is developed in every sense. The need becomes more and more frequent to interfere, to allay difficulties, to punish, or to coerce obedience; and thus develop the habit of rule and the usages of government. The two groups, separated to begin with, and then united on one territory, are at first merely laid alongside one another, then are scattered through one another like a mechanical mixture, as the term is used in chemistry, until gradually they become more and more of a "chemical combination." They intermingle, unite, amalgamate to unity, in customs and habits, in speech and worship. Soon the bonds of relationship unite the upper and the lower strata. In nearly all cases the master class picks the handsomest virgins from the subject races for its concubines. A race of bastards thus develops, sometimes taken into the ruling class, sometimes rejected, and then because of the blood of the masters in their veins, becoming the born leaders of the subject race. In form and in content the primitive State is completed.

III: The Primitive Feudal State

THE FORM OF DOMINION

Its form is domination; the dominion of a small warlike minority, interrelated and closely allied, over a definitely bounded territory and its cultivators. Gradually, custom develops some form of law in accordance with which this dominion is exercised. This law regulates the rights of primacy and the claims of the lords, and the duty of obedience and of service on the part of the subjects, in such wise that the capacity of the peasants for rendering service is not impaired. This word, *praestationsfaehigkeit* dates from the reforms of Frederick the Great. The "bee-keepership," therefore, is governed by the law of custom. The duty of paying and working on the part of the peasants corresponds to the duty of protection on the part of the lords, who ward off exactions of their own companions, as well as defend the peasants from the attacks of foreign enemies.

Although this is one part of the content of the State concept, there is another, which in the beginning is of much greater magnitude; the idea of economic exploitation, the political means for the satisfaction of needs. The peasant surrenders a portion of the product of his labor, without any equivalent service in return. *"In the beginning was the ground rent."*

The forms under which the ground rent is collected or consumed vary. In some cases, the lords, as a closed union or community, are settled in some fortified camp and consume as communists the tribute of their peasantry. This is the situation in the State of the Inca. In some cases, each individual warrior-noble has a definite strip of land assigned to him: but generally the product of this is still, as in Sparta, consumed in the "syssitia," by class associates and companions in arms. In some cases, the landed nobility scatters over the entire territory, each man housed with his following in his fortified castle, and consuming, each for himself, the produce of his dominion or lands.

As yet these nobles have not become landlords, in the sense that they administer their property. Each of them receives tribute from the labor of his dependents, whom he neither guides nor supervises. This is the type of the mediaeval dominion in the lands of the Germanic nobility. Finally, the knight becomes the owner and administrator of the knight's fee.[*] His former serfs develop into the laborers of his plantation, and the tribute now appears as the profit of the entrepreneur. This is the type of the earliest capitalist enterprise of modern times, the exploitation of large territories in the lands east of the Elbe, formerly occupied by Slavs and later colonized by Germans. Numerous transitions lead from one stage to the other.

But always, in its essence, is the "State" the same. Its purpose, in every case, is found to be the political means for the satisfaction of needs. At first, its method is by exacting a ground rent, so long as there exists no trade activity the products of which can be appropriated. Its form, in every case, is that of dominion, whereby exploitation is regarded as "justice," maintained as a "constitution," insisted on strictly, and in case of need enforced with cruelty. And yet, in these ways, the absolute right of the conqueror becomes narrowed within the confines of law, for the sake of permitting the continuous acquisition of ground rents. The duty of furnishing supplies on the part of the subjects is limited by their right to maintain themselves in good condition. The right of taxation on the part of the lords is supplemented by their duty to afford protection within and without the State—security under the law and defense of the frontier.

At this point, the primitive State is completely developed in all its essentials. It has passed the embryonic condition; whatever follows can be only phenomena of growth.

As compared with unions of families, the State represents, doubtless, a much higher species; since the State embraces a greater mass of men,

---

* *Rittergutsbesitz* is the ultimate molecule of the German feudal system, a non-urban territory, approximating the concept of knight's fee in the Angevin fiscal legislation; in modern Germanic law, the possession of an acreage, alienable only as an entity, and by recent legislation, alienable to non-nobles, but subject to and capable of certain exceptions in law not inhering in other forms of real estate.—*Translator.*

in closer articulation, more capable of conquering nature and of warding off enemies. It changes the half playful occupations of men into strict methodic labor, and thus brings untold misery to innumerable generations yet unborn. Henceforth, these must eat their bread in the sweat of their brow, since the golden age of the free community of blood relations has been followed by the iron rule of State dominion. But the State, by discovering labor in its proper sense, starts in this world that force which alone can bring about the golden age on a much higher plane of ethical relation and of happiness for all. The State, to use Schiller's words, destroys the untutored happiness of the people while they were children, in order to bring them along a sad path of suffering to the conscious happiness of maturity.

A higher species! Paul von Lilienfeld, one of the principal advocates of the view that society is an organism of a higher kind, has pointed out that in this respect an especially striking parallel can be drawn between ordinary organism and this super-organism. All higher beings propagate sexually; lower beings asexually, by partition, by budding and sometimes by conjugation. We have shown that simple partition corresponds exactly to the growth and the further development of the association based on blood relationship, which existed before the State. This grows until it becomes too large for cohesion; it then loses its unity, divides, and the separate hordes, if they associate at all, remain in a very loose connection, without any sort of closer articulation. The amalgamation of exogamic groups is comparable to conjugation.

The State, however, comes into being through sexual propagation. All bisexual propagation is accomplished by the following process: The male element, a small, very active, mobile, vibrating cell—the spermatozoon—searches out a large inactive cell without mobility of its own—the ovum, or female principle—enters and fuses with it. From this process, there results an immense growth; that is to say, a wonderful differentiation with simultaneous integration. The inactive peasantry, bound by nature to their fields, is the ovum, the mobile tribe of herdsmen the spermatozoon, of this sociologic act of fecundation; and its resultant is the ripening of a higher social organism more fully differentiated in its organs, and much more complete in its integrations. It is easy to find further parallels. One may compare the border feuds to the manner in which innumerable spermatozoa swarm about the ovum until finally one, the strongest or most fortunate, discovers and conquers the micropyle. One may compare the almost magical attraction which the ovum has for the spermatozoon, to the no less magical power by which the herdsmen from the steppes are drawn into the cultivated plains.

But all this is no proof for the "organism." The problem, however, has been pointed out.

THE INTEGRATION

We have followed the genesis of the State, from its second stage onward, in its objective growth as a political and jural form with economic content. But it is far more important to examine its subjective growth, its socio-psychological "differentiation and integration," since all sociology is nearly always social psychology. First, then, let us discuss integration.

We saw in the second stage, as set forth above, how the net of psychical relations becomes ever tighter and closer enmeshed, as the economic amalgamation advances. The two dialects become one language; or one of the two, often of an entirely different stock from the other, becomes extinct. This, in some cases, is the language of the victors, but more frequently that of the vanquished. Both cults amalgamate to one religion, in which the tribal god of the conquerors is adored as the principal divinity, while the old gods of the vanquished become either his servants, or, as demons or devils, his adversaries. The bodily type tends to assimilate, through the influence of the same climate and similar mode of living. Where a strong difference between the types existed or is maintained,[45] the bastards, to a certain extent, fill the gap—so that, in spite of the still existing ethnic contrast, everybody, more and more, begins to feel that the type of the enemies beyond the border is more strange, more "foreign" than is the new co-national type. Lords and subjects view one another as "we," at least as concerns the enemy beyond the border; and at length the memory of the different origin completely disappears. The conquerors are held to be the sons of the old gods. This, in many cases, they literally are, since these gods are nothing but the souls of their ancestors raised to godhead by apotheosis.

Since the new "States" are much more aggressive than the former communities bound together by mere blood relationship, the feeling of being different from the foreigner beyond the borders, growing in frequent feuds and wars, becomes stronger and stronger among those within the "realm of peace." And in the same measure there grows among them the feeling of belonging to another; so that the spirit of fraternity and of equity, which formerly existed only within the horde and which never ceased to hold sway within the association of nobles, takes root everywhere, and more and more finds its place in the relations between the lords and their subjects.

At first these relations are manifested only in infrequent cases: equity and fraternity are allowed only such play as is consistent with the right to use the political means; but that much is granted. A far stronger bond of psychical community between high and low, more potent than any success against foreign invasion, is woven by legal protection against the aggression of the mighty. *"Justitia fundamentum regnorum."* When, pursuant to their own ideas of justice, the aristocrats as a social group execute one of their own class for murder or robbery, for having exceeded the bounds of permitted exploitation, the thanks and the joy of the subjects are even more heartfelt than after victory over alien foes.

These, then, are the principal lines of development of the psychical integration. Common interest in maintaining order and law and peace produce a strong feeling of solidarity, which may be called "a consciousness of belonging to the same State."

THE DIFFERENTIATION: GROUP THEORIES AND GROUP PSYCHOLOGY

On the other hand, as in all organic growth, there develops *pari passu* a psychic differentiation just as powerful. The interests of the group produce strong group feelings; the upper and lower strata develop a "class consciousness" corresponding to their peculiar interests.

The separate interest of the master group is served by maintaining intact the imposed law of political means; such interest makes for "conservatism." The interest of the subject group, on the contrary, points to the removal of the prevailing rule, to the substitution for it of a new rule, the law of equality for all inhabitants of the State, and makes for "liberalism" and revolution.

Herein lies the tap root of all class and party psychology. Hence there develop, in accordance with definite psychological laws, those incomparably mighty forms of thought which, as "class theories," through thousands of years of struggle guide and justify every social contest in the consciousness of contemporaries.

"When the will speaks reason has to be silent," says Schopenhauer, or as Ludwig Gumplowicz states the same idea, "Man acts in accordance with laws of nature, as an after-thought he thinks humanly." Man's will being strictly "determined," he must act according to the pressure which the surrounding world exerts upon him; and the same law is valid for every community of men: groups, classes, and the State itself. They "flow from the plane of higher economic and social pressure to that of lower pressure, along the line of least resistance." But every individual and each community of men believe themselves free agents; and therefore, by an unescapable psychical law they are forced to consider the path they are traversing as a freely chosen means, and the point toward which they are driven as a freely chosen end. And since man is a rational and ethical being, that is, a social entity, he is obliged to justify before reason and morality the method and the objective point of his movement, and to take account of the social consciousness of his time.

So long as the relations of both groups were simply those of internationally opposed border enemies, the exercise of the political means called for no justification, because a man of alien blood had no rights. As soon, however, as the psychic integration develops, in any degree, the community feeling of State consciousness, as soon as the bond servant acquires "rights," and the consciousness of essential equality percolates through the mass, the political means requires a system of justification; and there arises in the ruling class the group theory of "legitimacy."

Everywhere, the upholders of legitimacy justify dominion and exploitation with similar anthropological and theological reasoning. The master group, since it recognizes bravery and warlike efficiency as the only virtues of a man, declares itself, the victors,—and from its standpoint quite correctly—to be the more efficient, the better "race." This point of view is the more intensified, the lower the subject race is reduced by hard labor and low fare. And since the tribal god of the ruling group has become the supreme god in the new amalgamated State religion, this religion declares—and again from its view-point quite correctly—that the constitution of the State has been decreed by heaven, that it is "tabu," and that interference with it is sacrilege. In consequence, therefore, of a simple logical inversion, the exploited or subject group is regarded as an essentially inferior race, as unruly, tricky, lazy, cowardly and utterly incapable of self-rule or self-defense, so that any uprising against the imposed dominion must necessarily appear as a revolt against God Himself and against His moral ordinances. For these reasons, the dominant group at all times stands in closest union with the priesthood, which, in its highest positions, at least, nearly always recruits itself from their sons, sharing their political rights and economic privileges.

This has been, and is at this day, the class theory of the ruling group; nothing has been taken from it, not an item has been added to it. Even the very modern argument by which, for example, the landed nobility of old France and of modern Prussia attempted to put out of court the claims of the peasantry to the ownership of lands, on the allegation that they had owned the land from time immemorial, while their peasants had only been granted a life tenure therein,—is reproduced among the Wahuma, of Africa,[46] and probably could be shown in many other instances.

Like their class theory, their class psychology has been, and is, at all times the same. Its most important characteristic, the "aristocrat's pride," shows itself in contempt for the lower laboring strata. This is so inherent, that herdsmen, even after they have lost their herds and become economically dependent, still retain their pride as former lords: "Even the Galla, who had been despoiled of their wealth of herds by the Somali north of the Tana, and who thus have become watchers of other men's herds, and even in some cases along the Sabaki become peasants, still look with contempt upon the peasant Watokomo, who are subject to them and resemble the Suaheli. But their attitude is quite different toward their tributary hunting peoples, namely, the Waboni, the Wassanai, and the Walangulo (Ariangulo) who resemble the Galla."[47]

The following description of the Tibbu applies, as though it had been originally told of them, to Walter Havenaught and the rest of the poor knights who, in the crusades, looked for booty and lordly domain. It applies no less to many a noble fighting cock from Germany east of the Elbe, and to many a ragged Polish gentleman. "They are men full of self-consciousness. They may be beggars, but they are no pariahs. Many a people under these circumstances would be thoroughly miserable and depressed; the Tibbu have steel in their nature. They are splendidly fitted to be robbers, warriors, and rulers. Even their system of robbery is imposing, although it is base as a jackal's. These ragged Tibbus, fighting against extreme poverty and constantly on the verge of starvation, raise the most impudent claims with apparent or real belief in their validity. The right of the jackal, which regards the possessions of a stranger as common property, is the protection of greedy men against want. The insecurity of an all but perpetual state of war brings it about that life becomes an insistent challenge, and at the same time the reward of extortion!"[48] This phenomenon is in nowise limited to Eastern Africa, for it is said of the Abyssinian soldier: "Thus equipped he comes along. Proudly he looks down on every one: his is the land, and for him the peasant must work."[49]

Deeply as the aristocrat at all times despises the economic means and the peasants who employ it, he admits frankly his reliance on the political means. Honest war and "honest thievery"* are his occupation as a lord, are his good right. His right—except over those who belong to the same clique—extends just as far as his power. One finds this high praise of the political means nowhere so well stated as in the well-known Doric drinking song:

> I have great treasures; the spear and the sword;
>   Wherewith to guard my body, the bull hide shield well tried.
> With these I can plough, and harvest my crop,
>   With these I can garner the sweet grape wine,
> By them I bear the name "Lord" with my serfs.
>
>   But these never dare to bear spear and sword,
> Still less the guard of the body, the bull hide shield well tried.
>   They lie at my feet stretched out on the ground,
>   My hand is licked by them as by hounds,
>   I am their Persian king—terrifying them by my name.[50]

In these wanton lines is expressed the pride of warlike lords. The following verses, taken from an entirely different phase of civilization, show that the robber still has part in the warrior in spite of Christianity, the Peace of God, and the Holy Roman Empire of the German Nation. These lines also praise the political means, but in its most crude form, simple robbery:

---

* Compare this with the prevalent justification of "honest graft" in municipal or political contracts.—*Translator.*

Would you eke out your life, my young noble squire,
   Follow then my teaching, upon your horse and join the gang!
Take to the greenwood, when the peasant comes up,
   Run him down quickly, grab him then by the collar,
Rejoice in your heart, taking from him whatever he has,
   Unharness his horses and get you away![51]

"Unless," as Sombart adds "he preferred to hunt nobler game and to relieve merchants of their valuable consignments." The nobles carried on robbery as a natural method of supplementing their earnings, extending it more and more as the income from their property no longer sufficed to pay for the increasing demands of daily consumption and luxury. The system of freebooting was considered a thoroughly honorable occupation, since it met the demand of the essence of chivalry, that every one should appropriate whatever was within reach of his spear point or of the blade of his sword. The nobles learned freebooting as the cobbler was brought up to his trade. The ballad has put this in merry wise:

To pillage, to rob, that is no shame,
The best in the land do quite the same.

Besides this principal point of the "squire-archical" psychology, a second distinguishing mark scarcely less characteristic is found in the piety of these folk whether it be of conviction or merely strongly accentuated in public.

It seems as though the same social ideas always force identical characteristics on the ruling class. This is illustrated by the form under which God, in their view, appears as their special National God and preponderatingly as a God of War. Although they profess God as the creator of all men, even of their enemies, and since Christianity, as the God of Love, this does not counteract the force with which class interests formulate their appropriate ideology.

In order to complete the sketch of the psychology of the ruling class, we must not forget the tendency to squander, easily understood in those "ignorant of the taste of toil," which appears sometimes in a higher form as generosity; nor must we forget, as their supreme trait, that death-despising bravery, which is called forth by the coercion imposed on a minority, their need to defend their rights at any time with arms, and which is favored by a freedom from all labor which permits the development of the body in hunting, sport and feuds. Its caricature is combativeness, and a super-sensitiveness to personal honor, which degenerates into madness.

At this point a small digression: Caesar found the Celts just at that stage of their development, in which the nobles had obtained dominion over their fellow clansmen. Since that time, his classic narrative has stood as a norm—their class psychology appears as the race psychology of all Celts. Not even Mommsen escaped this error. The result is that now, in every book on universal history or sociology, one may read the palpable error, repeated until contradiction is of no avail, although a mere glance would have sufficed to show that all peoples of all races, in the same stage of their development, have showed the same characteristics; in Europe, Thessalians, Apulians, Campanians, Germans, Poles, etc. Meanwhile the Celts, and specifically the French, in different stages of their development, have showed quite different traits of character. The psychology belongs to the stage of development, not to the race!

Whenever, on the other hand, the religious sanctions of the "State" are weak, or become so, there develops as a group theory on the part of the subjects, the concept, either clear or blurred, of *Natural Law*. The lower class regards the race pride and the assumed superiority of the nobles as presumptuous, claims to be of as good race and blood as the ruling class—and from their standpoint again quite correctly, since according to their views, labor, efficiency and order are accounted the only virtues. They are skeptical also as to the religion which is the helper of their adversaries; and are as firmly convinced as are the nobles of the directly opposite opinion, namely, that the privileges of the master group violate law as well as reason. Later development is not able to add any essential point to the factors originally given.

Under the influence of these ideas, now clearly, now obscurely brought out, the two groups henceforth fight out their battles, each for its own interests. The young State would be burst apart under the strain of such centrifugal forces, were it not for the centripetal pull of common interests, of the still more powerful State-consciousness. The pressure of foreigners from without, of common enemies, overcomes the inner strain of conflicting class interests. An example may be found in the tale of the secession of the "Plebs" and the successful mission of Menenius Agrippa. And so the young State would, like a planet, swing through all eternity in its predetermined orbit, in accordance with the parallelogram of forces, were it not that it and its surrounding world is changed and developed until it produces new external and inner energies.

THE PRIMITIVE FEUDAL STATE OF HIGHER GRADE

Growth in itself conditions important changes; and the young State must grow. The same forces that brought it into being, urge its extension, require it to grasp more power. Even were such a young State "sated," as many a modern State claims to be, it would still be forced to stretch and grow under penalty of extinction. Under primitive social conditions Goethe's lines apply with absolute truth: "You must rise or fall, conquer or yield, be hammer or anvil."

States are maintained in accordance with the same principles that called them into being. The primitive State is the creation of warlike robbery; and only by warlike robbery can it be preserved.

The economic want of the master group has no limits; no man is sufficiently rich to satisfy his desires. The political means are turned on new groups of peasants not yet subjected, or new coasts yet unpilfered are sought out. The primitive State expands, until a collision takes place on the edge of the "sphere of interests" of another primitive State, which itself originated in precisely the same way. Then we have for the first time, in place of the warlike robbery heretofore carried on, true war in its narrower sense, since henceforth equally organized and disciplined masses are hurled at one another.

The object of the contest remains always the same, the produce of the economic means of the working classes, such as loot, tribute, taxes and ground rent; but the contest no longer takes place between a group intent on exploiting and another mass to be exploited, but between two master groups for the possession of the entire booty.

The final result of the conflict, in nearly all instances, is the amalgamation of both primitive States into a greater. This in turn, naturally and by force of the same causes, reaches beyond its borders, devours its smaller neighbors, and is perhaps in its turn devoured by some greater State.

The subjected laboring group may not take much interest in the final issue of these contests for the mastery; it is a matter of indifference whether it pays tribute to one or the other set of lords. Their chief interest lies in the course of the particular fight, which is, in any case, paid for with their own hides. Therefore, except in cases of gross ill treatment and exploitation, the lower classes are rightly governed by their "State-consciousness" when, with all their might they aid their hereditary master group in times of war. For if their master group is vanquished, the subjects suffer most severely from the utter devastation of war. They fight literally for wife and children, for home and hearth, when they fight to prevent the rule of foreign masters.

The master group is involved completely in the issue of this fight for dominion. In extreme cases, it may be completely exterminated, as were the local nobility of the Germanic tribes in the Frankish Empire. Nearly as bad, if not worse, is the prospect of being thrust into the group of the serfs. Sometimes, a well-timed treaty of peace preserves their social position as master groups of subordinate rank: e.g., the Saxon nobility in Norman England, or the Suppans in German territory taken from the Slavs. In other cases, where the forces are about equal, the two groups amalgamate into one master group with equal rights, which forms a nobility whose members intermarry. This, for instance, was the situation in the Slavic Territories, where isolated Wendish chieftains were treated as the equals of the Germans, or in mediaeval Rome, in the case of prominent families from the Alban Hills and Tuscany.

In this new "primitive feudal State of higher grade," as we shall call it, the ruling group may, therefore, disintegrate into a number of more or less powerful and privileged strata. The organization may show many varieties because of the well-known fact, that often the master group separates into two subordinated economic and social layers, developed as we saw them in the herdsmen stage: the owners of large herds and of many slaves, and the ordinary freemen. Possibly the less complete differentiation into social ranks in the States created by huntsmen in the new world, is to be assigned to the circumstance that in the absence of herds, the concomitants of that form of ownership, and the original separation into classes, were not introduced into the State. We shall, later, see what force was exerted on the political and economic development of States in the old world by the differences in rank and property of the two strata of rulers.

Similarly, as in the case of the ruling group, a corresponding process of differentiation divides the subject group in the "primitive feudal State of a higher grade" into various strata more or less despised; and compelled to render service. It is only necessary to recall the very marked difference in the social and jural position occupied by the peasantry in the Doric States, Lacedaemon and Crete, and among the Thessalians, where the perioiki had clear rights of possession and fairly well protected political rights, while the helots, in the latter case the *penestai*, were almost unprotected in life and property. Among the old Saxons also we find a class, the liti, intermediate between the common freemen and the serfs.[52] These examples could be multiplied; apparently they are caused by the same tendencies that brought about the differentiation among the nobility mentioned above. When two primitive feudal States amalgamate, their social layers stratify in a variety of ways, which to a certain extent are comparable to the combinations resulting from mixing together two packs of cards.

It is certain that this mechanical mixture caused by political forces, influences the development of *castes*, that is to say, of hereditary professions, which at the same time form a hierarchy of social classes. "Castes are usually, if not always, consequences of conquest and subjugation by foreigners."[53] Although this problem has not been completely solved, it may be said that the formation of castes has been very strongly influenced by economic and religious factors. It is probable that castes came about in some such way as this: State-forming forces penetrated into existing economic organizations, and vocations underwent adaptation, and then became petrified under the influence of religious concepts, which, however, may also have influenced their original formation. This seems to follow from the fact that even as between man and woman there exist certain separations of vocation, which, so to say, are taboo and impassable. Thus among all huntsmen, tilling the ground is woman's work, while among many African shepherds, as soon as the ox-plow is used, agriculture becomes man's work, and then women may not, under pain of sacrilege, use the domestic cattle.[*]

It is likely that such religious concepts may have brought it about that a vocation became hereditary, and then compulsorily hereditary, especially where a tribe or a village carried on a particular craft. This happens with all tribes in a state of nature, where intercourse is easily possible,

---

[*] Similarly there are North Asiatic tribes of huntsmen, where women are definitely forbidden to touch the hunting gear or to cross a hunting trail.— Ratzel I, page 650.

especially in the case of islanders. When some such group has been
conquered by another tribe, the subjects, with their developed hereditary vocations, tend to form within the new State entity a pure "caste."
Their caste position depends partly upon the esteem they had heretofore
enjoyed among their own people, and partly upon the advantage which
their vocation affords their new masters. If, as was often the case, waves
of conquest followed one another in series, the formation of castes might
be multiplied, especially if in the meantime economic development had
worked out many vocational classes.

This development is probably best seen in the group of smiths,
who, in nearly all cases, have occupied a peculiar position, half feared
and half despised. In Africa especially, since the beginning of time,
we find tribes of expert smiths, as followers and dependents of
shepherd tribes. The Hyksos brought such tribes with them into the
Nile country, and perhaps owed their decisive victory to arms made
by them; and until recent times the Dinka kept the iron working Djur
in a sort of subject relation. The same applied also to the nomads of
the Sahara; while our northern sagas are filled with the tribal contrast
to the "dwarfs" and the fear of their magical powers. All the elements
were at hand in a developed State for the formation of sharply
differentiated castes.[54]

How the cooperation of religious concepts affects the beginning of
these formations may be well illustrated by an example from Polynesia.
Here, "although many natives have the ability to do ship-building, only
one privileged class may exercise the craft, so closely is the interest of
the States and the societies bound up in this art. All over the archipelago
formerly, and to this day in Fiji, the carpenters, who are almost
exclusively ship-builders, form a special caste, bear the high sounding
title of 'the king's workmen', and enjoy the prerogative of having their
own chieftains. . . . Everything is done in accordance with ancient
tradition; the laying the keel, the completion of the ship, and the
launching, all take place amidst religious ceremonies and feasts."[55]

Where superstition has been strongly developed, a genuine system of
castes may come about, based partly on economic and partly on ethnic
foundations. In Polynesia, for example, the articulation of the classes,
through the operation of the taboo, has brought about a State of affairs
very like a most thorough-going caste system.[56] Similar results may be
seen in Southern Arabia.[57] It is unnecessary at this place to enlarge on

the important place which religion had in the origin and maintenance of separate castes in ancient Egypt and in modern India.[*]

These are the elements of the primitive feudal State of higher grade. They are more manifold and more numerous than in the lower primitive State; but in both, legal constitution and political-economic distribution are fundamentally the same. The products of the economic means are still the object of the group struggle. This remains now as ever the moving impulse of the domestic policy of the State, while the political means continues now as ever to constitute the moving impulse of its foreign policy in attack or in defense. Identical group theories continue to justify, both for the upper classes and the lower, the objects and means of external and domestic struggles.

But the development can not remain stationary. Growth differs from mere increase in bulk; growth means a constantly heightening differentiation and integration.

The farther the primitive feudal State extends its dominion, the more numerous its subjects, and the denser its population, the more there develops a political-economic division of labor, which calls forth new needs and new means of supplying them; and the more there come into sharp contrasts the distinctions of economic, and consequently of social, class strata, in accordance with what I have called the "law of the agglomeration about existing nuclei of wealth." This growing differentiation becomes decisive for the further development of the primitive feudal State, and still more for its conclusion.

This conclusion is not meant to be, in any sense, the physical end of such a State. We do not mean the death of a State, whereby such a feudal State of the higher type disappears, in consequence of conflict with a more powerful State, either on the same or on a higher plane of development, as was the case of the Mogul States of India or of Uganda in their conflicts with Great Britain. Neither does it mean such a stagnation as that into which Persia and Turkey have fallen, which represents for a time only a pause in development, since these countries,

---

[*] Besides, it seems that the rigidity of the Indian caste-system is not so harsh in practice. The guild seems as often to break through the barriers of caste as the converse.—Ratzel II, page 596.

either of their own force or by foreign conquest, must soon be pushed on the way of their destiny. Neither have we meant the rigidity of the gigantic Chinese Empire, which can last only so long as foreign powers refrain from forcing its mysterious gates.[*]

The outcome here spoken of means the further development of the primitive feudal State, a matter of importance to our understanding of universal history as a *process*. The principal lines of development into which this issue branches off are twofold and of fundamentally different character. *But this polar opposition is conditioned by a like contrast between two sorts of economic wealth each of which increases in accordance with the "law of agglomeration about existing nuclei."* In the one case, it is movable property; in the other, landed property. Here it is the capital of commerce, there property in land, accumulating in the hands of a smaller and smaller number, and thereby overturning radically the articulation of classes, and with it the whole State.

The maritime State is the scene of the development of movable wealth; the territorial State is the embodiment of the development of landed property. The final issue of the first is *capitalistic exploitation* by slavery, the outcome of the latter is, first of all, the *developed feudal State*.

Capitalistic exploitation by slavery, the typical result of the development of the so-called "antique States" on the Mediterranean, does not end in the death of States, which is of no importance, but in the death of peoples, because of the consumption of population. In the pedigree of the historical development of the State, it forms a side branch, from which no further immediate growth can take place.

The developed feudal State, however, represents the principal branch, the continuation of the trunk; and is therefore the origin for the further

---

[*] Had we the space, a detailed exposition of this exceptional development of a feudal State would be tempting. China would be well worth a more detailed discussion, since, in many aspects it has approached the condition of "free citizenship" more closely than any people of Western Europe. China has overcome the consequences of the feudal system more thoroughly than we Europeans have; and has made, early in its development, the great property interests in the land harmless, so that their bastard offspring, capitalism hardly came into being; while in addition, it has worked out to a considerable degree the problems of cooperative production and of cooperative distribution.

growth of the State. Thence it has developed into the State governed by feudal systems; into absolutism; into the modern constitutional State; and if we are right in our prognosis, it will become a "free citizenship."

So long as the trunk grew only in one direction, i.e., to include the primitive feudal State of higher grade, our sketch of its growth and development could and did comprise both forms. Henceforth, after the bifurcation, our story branches and follows each branch to its last twig.

We begin, then, with the maritime States, although they are not the older form. On the contrary, as far back as the dawn of history clears the fog of prehistoric existence, the first strong States were formed as territorial States, which then, by their own powers, attained the scale of developed feudal States. But beyond this stage, at least as regards those States most interesting to our culture, most of them either remained stationary or fell into the power of maritime States; and then, infected with the deadly poison of capitalistic exploitation through slavery, were destroyed by the same plague.

The further progress of the expanded feudal States of higher grade could take place only after the maritime States had run their course: mighty forms of domination and Statescraft these became, and they subsequently influenced and furthered the conformation of the territorial States that grew from their ruins.

For that reason the story of the fate of maritime States must be first traced, as these are the introduction to the higher forms of State life. After first tracing the lateral branch, we shall then return to the starting point, the primitive feudal State, follow the main trunk to the development of the modern constitutional State, and anticipating actual history, sketch the "free citizenship" of the future.

IV: The Maritime State

The course of life and the path of suffering of the State founded by sea nomads, as has been stated above, is determined by commercial capital; just as that of the territorial State is determined by capital vested in realty; and, we may add, that of the modern constitutional State by productive capital. The sea nomad, however, did not invent trade or merchandising, fairs or markets or cities; these preexisted, and since they served his purpose were now developed to suit his interests. All these institutions, serving the economic means, the barter for equivalents, had long since been discovered.

Here for the first time in our survey we find the economic means not the object of exploitation by the political means, but as a cooperating agent in originating the State, one might call it the "chain" passing into the "lift" created by the feudal State to bring forth a more elaborate structure. The genesis of the maritime State would not be thoroughly intelligible, were we not to premise a statement concerning traffic and interchange of wares into prehistoric times. Furthermore, no prognosis of the modern State is complete, which does not take into account the independently formed economic means of aboriginal barter.

TRAFFIC IN PREHISTORIC TIMES

The psychological explanation of barter has brought forth the theory of the marginal utility, its greatest merit. According to this theory, the subjective valuation of any economic good decreases in proportion to the number of objects of the same kind possessed by the same owner. When even two proprietors meet, each having a number of similar articles, they will gladly barter, provided political means are barred, i.e., if both parts are apparently equally strong and well-armed, or in the very early stage, are within the sacred circle of relationship. By barter, each one receives property of very high subjective value, in place of property of very low subjective value, so that both parties are gainers in the transaction. The desire of primitive people for bartering must be stronger than that of cultured ones. For at this stage man does not value his own goods, but covets the things belonging to strangers, and is hardly affected by calculated economic considerations.

On the other hand, we must not forget that there are primitive peoples for whom barter has no attraction whatever. "Cook tells of tribes in Polynesia, with whom no intercourse was possible, since presents made absolutely no impression on them, and were afterward thrown away; everything shown them they regarded with indifference, and with no desire to own it, while with their own things they would not part; in fact, they had no conception of either trade or barter."[58] So Westermarck is of the opinion that "barter and traffic are comparatively late inventions." In this he stands in opposition to Peschel, who would have it that man in the earliest known stage of development engaged in barter. Westermarck states that there is no proof "that the cave-dwellers of Périgord from the reindeer period obtained their rock-crystals, their shells from the Atlantic, and the horns of the Saiga antelope from (modern) Poland by way of barter."[59]

In spite of these exceptions, which admit other explanations—perhaps the natives feared sorcery—the history of primitive peoples shows that the desire to trade and barter is a universal human characteristic. It can, however, take effect only when these primitive men on meeting with strangers are offered new enticing objects, since in the immediate circle of their own blood kinsmen every one has the same kinds of property, and in their natural communism, on the average about the same amount.

Yet even then, barter, the beginning of all regular trading, can take place only when the meeting with foreigners is a peaceable one. But is there any possibility for peaceable meeting with foreigners? Is not primitive man, through his entire life, and especially at the period when barter begins, still under the apprehension that every one of a different horde is an enemy to be feared as the wolf?

After trade is developed, it is, as a rule, strongly influenced by the "political means," "trade generally follows robbery."[60] But its first beginnings are chiefly the result of the economic means, the outcome of pacific, not warlike, intercourse.

The international relations of primitive huntsmen with one another must not be confused with those existing either between the huntsmen or herdsmen and their peasants, or amongst the herdsmen themselves. There are, undoubtedly, blood-feuds, or feuds because of looted women, or possibly because of violation of the districts set aside for hunting grounds; but these lack that strong incentive, which is the consequence of avarice alone, of the desire to despoil other men of the products of their labor. Therefore, the "wars" of primitive huntsmen are scarcely real wars, but rather scuffles and single combats, carried on frequently—as are the German student duels—according to an established ceremonial, and prolonged only up to the point of incapacity to fight, as one might say, "until claret has been drawn."[61] These tribes, numerically very weak, wisely limit bloodshed to the indispensable amount—e.g., in case of a blood vendetta feud—and thus avoid starting new vendetta blood feuds.

For this reason, pacific relations with their neighbors on an equal economic scale are much stronger, and also freer from the incentive to use political means, both among huntsmen and among primitive peasants, than among herdsmen. There are numerous examples where the former meet peaceably to exploit natural resources in common. "While yet in primitive stages of civilization, great masses of people gather together, from time to time, at places where useful objects may be found. The Indians of a large part of America made regular pilgrimages to the flint grounds; others assembled annually at harvest time at the Zizania swamps of the lakes of the Northwest. The Australians, living scattered in the Barku district, assemble from all directions for the harvest festivals at the swamp beds of the corn bearing Marsiliacae."[62] "When the bonga-bonga trees in Queensland produce a superabundant crop, and a greater store is on hand than the tribe can consume, foreign tribes are permitted to share therein."[63] "Various tribes agree on the common ownership of definite strips of territory, and likewise of the quarries of phonolite for hatchets."[64] Numerous Australian tribes have common consultations and sessions of the elders for judgment. In these, the remainder of the population form the bystanders, a custom similar to the Germanic *"Umstand"* in the primitive folkmoot.[65]

It is but natural that such meetings should bring about barter. Perhaps this explains the origin of those "weekly fairs held by the Negroes of Central Africa in the midst of the primaeval forest *under special arrangements for the peace,*"[66] and likewise the great fairs, said to be very ancient, of the fur hunters of the extreme north of the Tschuktsche.

All these things presuppose the development of pacific forms of intercourse between neighboring groups. These forms are to be found almost universally. They could very easily be developed at this period, since the discovery had not yet been made that men can be utilized as labor motors. At this stage, the stranger is treated as an enemy only in doubtful cases. If he comes with apparently peaceable intent, he is treated as a friend. Therefore, a whole code of public law ceremonies grew up, intended to demonstrate the pacific intent of the newcomer.* One puts aside one's arms and shows one's unarmed hand, or one sends heralds in advance, who are always inviolable.[67]

It is clear that these forms represent some kind of claim to hospitality, and in fact it is by this guest-right that peaceful trade is first made possible. The exchange of guest-gifts precedes, and appears to introduce, barter proper. It becomes, therefore, important to investigate the source of hospitality.

Westermarck, in his recent monumental work (1907), *Origin and Development of Moral Concepts,*[68] states that the custom of hospitality results from two causes, curiosity for news from the stranger from afar, and still more from the fear that the stranger may be endowed with powers of sorcery, imputed to him just because he is a stranger.[†] In the Bible, hospitality is recommended for the reason that one can not know that the stranger may not be an angel. The superstitious race fears his curse (the Erinys of the Greeks) and hastens to propitiate the stranger. Having been accepted as a guest he is inviolable and enjoys the sacred right of the blood-related group, and is regarded as belonging to it during his stay. Therefore he partakes of the benefits of the aboriginal commu-

---

* In this category must be reckoned the salutation, still in use in some parts, "Peace Be With You." It is expressive of the perversity of Tolstoi's later years that he misapprehends this characteristic mark of a time when war was the normal state of affairs, as the remnant of a golden age of peace. *The Importance of the Russian Revolution* (German translation by A. Hess, p. 17).

† This may account for the use made of old women as heralds. They are doubly available for that purpose, since they are worthless for warfare, and are supposed to be endowed with specific powers of sorcery (Westermarck), even more than old men, who are also treated cautiously, since they may soon become "ghosts."

nism reigning in the group, and shares its property. The host demands
and receives whatever he claims, the stranger obtains in turn what he
asks for. When the peaceable intercourse becomes more frequent, the
mutual giving of guest-presents may develop into a trading arrangement,
because the trader gladly returns to the spot where he found good
entertainment and a profitable exchange and where he is protected by
the laws of hospitality, instead of seeking new places, where, often with
danger to his life, he would first have to acquire the right to hospitality.

The existence of an "international" division of labor is, of course
presupposed before the development of a regular trade relation can
begin. Such a division of labor exists much earlier and to a greater extent
than is generally believed. "It is quite erroneous to suppose that the
division of labor takes place only on a high scale of economic development. There are in the interior of Africa villages of iron-smiths, nay, of
such as only turn out dart-knives; New Guinea has its villages of potters,
North America its arrow-head makers."[69] From such specialties there
develops trade, whether through roving merchants, or by gifts to one's
hosts, or by peace-gifts from tribe to tribe. In North America, the Kaddu
trade in bows. "Obsidian was universally employed for arrow heads and
knives; on the Yellowstone, on the Snake River, in New Mexico, but
especially in Mexico. Thence the precious article was distributed all over
the entire country as far as Ohio and Tennessee, a distance of nearly two
thousand miles."[70]

According to Vierkandt: "From the purely home-made products of
primitive peoples, there results a system of trade totally distinct from that
prevailing under modern conditions. . . . Each separate tribe has
developed special aptitudes, leading to interexchange. Even among the
comparatively uncivilized Indian tribes of South America, we find such
differentiations. . . . By such a trade, products may be distributed over
extraordinary distances, not in any direct way through professional
traders, but through a gradual passing along from tribe to tribe. The
origin of such a trade, as Buecher has shown, is to be traced back to the
exchange of guest-gifts."[71]

Besides this exchange of guest-gifts, a trade may grow from the peace
offerings which adversaries after a fight exchange as a sign of reconcili-
ation. Sartorius reports on Polynesia: "After a war between different
islands, the peace offerings for each group were something novel; and
if the present and return present pleased both parties, a repetition took

place, and thus again the way for exchange of products was opened. But, these, in contrast to guest-gifts, were the bases of continuing intercourse. Here, in place of the contact of individuals, tribes and peoples met. Women are the first object of barter; they form the connecting link between strange tribes, and according to evidence from many sources, women are exchanged for cattle."[72]

We meet here an object of trade, exchangeable even without "international division of labor." And it appears as though the *exchange of women* had, in many ways, smoothed the way for the traffic in merchandise, as though it had been the first step toward the *peaceable* integration of tribes, which accompanied the *warlike* integration of the formation of the State. Lippert, however, believes that the peaceful *exchange of fire* antedates this barter.[73] Conceding that this custom is very ancient, he can nevertheless trace it only from rudiments of observances and of law; and since proof is no longer accessible, we shall not pursue the question further in this place.

On the other hand, the exchange of women is observed universally, and doubtless exerts an extraordinarily strong influence in the development of peaceable intercourse between neighboring tribes, and in the preparation for barter of merchandise. The story of the Sabine women, who threw themselves between their brothers and their husbands, as these were about to engage in battle, must have been an actuality in a thousand instances in the course of the development of the human race. All over the world, the marriage of near relatives is considered an outrage, as "incest," for reasons not within the scope of this book.[74] This directs the sexual longing toward the women of neighboring tribes, and thus makes the loot of women a part of the primary intertribal relations; and in nearly all cases, unless strong feelings of race counteract it, the violent carrying off of women is gradually commuted to barter and purchase, the custom resulting from the relative undesirability of the women of one's own blood in comparison to the wives to be had from other tribes.

Where division of labor made at all possible the exchange of goods, the relations among the various tribes would thereafter be made serviceable to it; the exogamic groups gradually become accustomed regularly to meet on a peaceful basis. The peace, originally protecting the horde of blood relations, thereafter comes to be extended over a wider circle. One example from numberless instances: "Each of the two

Camerun tribes has its own 'bush countries,' places where its own tribesmen trade, and where, by intermarriage, they have relatives. Here also exogamy shows its tribe-linking power."[75]

These are the principal lines of growth of peaceful barter and traffic; from the right to hospitality and the exchange of women, perhaps also from the exchange of fire, to the trade in commodities. In addition to this, markets and fairs, and perhaps also traders, were almost uniformly regarded as being under the protection of a god who preserved peace and avenged its violation. Thus we have brought the fundamentals of this most important sociological factor to the point where the political means enters as a cause to disturb, rearrange, and then to develop and affect the creations of the economic means.

TRADE AND THE PRIMITIVE STATE

There are two very important reasons why the robber-warrior should not unduly interfere with such markets and fairs as he may find within his conquered domain.

The first, which is extra-economic, is the superstitious fear that the godhead will avenge a breach of the peace. The second, which is economic, and probably is the more important—and I think I am the first to point out this connection—is that the conquerors can not well do without the markets.

The booty of the primitive victors consists of much property which is unavailable for their immediate use and consumption. Since valuable articles at that period exist in but few forms, while these few occur in large quantity, the "marginal utility" of any one kind is held very low. This applies especially to the most important product of the political means, slaves. Let us first take up the case of the herdsman: his need of slaves is limited by the size of his herds; he is very likely to exchange his surplus for other objects of greater value to him: for salt, ornaments, arms, metals, woven materials, utensils, etc. For that reason, the herdsman is not only at all times a robber, always in addition he is a merchant and trader and he protects trade.

He protects trade coming his way in order to exchange his loot against the products of another civilization—from the earliest times, nomads have convoyed the caravans passing through their steppes or deserts in consideration of protection money—but he also protects trade even in places conquered by him in prehistoric times. Quite the same sort of consideration which influenced the herdsmen to change from bear stage to bee-keeper stage, must have influenced them to maintain and protect ancient markets and fairs. One single looting, in this case, would mean killing the hen that lays the golden eggs. It is more profitable to preserve the market and rather to extend the prevailing peace over it, since there is not only the profit to be had from an exchange of foreign wares against loot, but also the protection money, the lords' toll, to be collected. For that reason princes of feudal States of every stage of development extended over markets, highways and merchants, their especial protection, the "king's peace," often indeed reserving to themselves the monopoly of foreign trade. Everywhere we see them busily engaged in calling into being new fairs and cities by the grant of protection and immunity.

This interest in the system of fairs and markets makes it thoroughly credible that tribes of herdsmen respected existing market places in their sphere of influence to such an extent that they suspended the exertion of the political means so completely as not even to exercise "dominion" over them. The story told by Herodotus is inherently probable, though he was astonished that the Argippaeans had a sacred market amidst the lawless Scythian herdsmen, and that their unarmed inhabitants were effectively protected through the hallowed peace of their market place. Many similar phenomena make this the more easily believable.

"No one dare harm them, since they are considered *holy*; and yet they have no arms; but it is they who allay the quarrels of their neighbors, and whoever has escaped to them as a runaway may not be touched by any other man."[76] Similar instances are found frequently: "It is always the same story of the Argippaeans, the story of the 'holy,' 'unarmed,' 'just,' bartering, and strife-setting tribelet in the midst of a Bedouin-like, nomadic population."[77] Caere may be taken as an example of a higher type. Strabo says of its inhabitants: "The Greeks thought highly of their bravery and justice, because although powerful in a great degree, they abstained from robbery." Mommsen, who quotes this passage, adds: "This does not exclude piracy, which was engaged in by the merchants of Caere as well as by all other merchants, but rather that Caere was a sort of free harbor for the Phoenicians as for the Greeks."[78]

Caere is not like the fair of the Argippaeans, a market place in the interior of a district of land nomads, but is in the midst *of a domain of sea nomads, a port endowed with its own peace*. This is one of those typical

formations whose importance, in my estimation, has not been appreciated at its real value. They have, it seems to me, exercised a mighty
influence on the genesis of maritime States.

Those reasons by which we saw the land nomads forced to preserve,
if not to create, market places, must with even more intensity, have
coerced the sea nomads to similar demeanor. For the transportation of
loot, especially of herds and of slaves, is difficult and dangerous on the
trails across the desert or the steppes: the slow progress invites pursuit.
But with war-canoe and "dragon-ship" this transportation is easy and
safe. For that reason, the Viking is even much more a trader and
merchant than is the herdsman. As is said in *Faust*, "War, Commerce,
and Piracy are inseparable."

THE GENESIS OF THE MARITIME STATE

In many cases, I believe, trade in the loot of piracy is the origin of those
cities around which, as political centers, the city-States of the antique
or Mediterranean civilization grew up; while in very many other cases,
the same trade cooperated to bring them to the same point of political
development.

These harbor markets developed from probably two general types:
they grew up either as piratical fortresses directly and intentionally placed
in hostile territory, or else as "merchant colonies" based on treaty rights
in the harbors of foreign primitive or developed feudal States.

Of the first type, we have a number of important examples from
ancient history which correspond exactly to the fourth stage of our
scheme, where an armed colony of pirates plants itself down at a
commercially and strategically defendable point on the seacoast of a
foreign State. The most notable instance is Carthage; and in like manner,
the Greek sea nomads, Ionians, Dorians and Achaeans, settled in their
sea castles on the Adriatic and Tyrrhenian coasts of Southern Italy, on
the islands of these seas, and on the gulfs of Southern Gaul. Phoenicians,
Etruscans,[*] Greeks, and according to modern investigation, Carians, all

---

[*] Whether the Etruscans were immigrants into Italy by land who took up piracy after
having made war successfully on land, or whether as sea nomads they had already
settled the country along the sea named after them, has not been determined.

about the Mediterranean, founded their "States" after the same type, with identical class division into masters and servile peasantry of the neighboring territory.[79]

Some of these States on the coast developed into feudal States of the type of the territorial States; and the master class then became a landed aristocracy. The factors in this change were: first, geographical conditions, lack of good harbors, and a wide stretch of *hinterland* cultivated by peaceful peasants; and secondly, very probably, the acquired organization into classes taken with them from their original homes. In many cases, they were fugitive nobles, the vanquished of domestic feuds, or younger sons, sometimes an entire generation of youth of both sexes, who thus started "on the viking," and having at home had lands and serfs, as petty lords, they again sought in foreign lands what they regarded as their due. The occupation of England by the Anglo-Saxons, and of Southern Italy by the Normans, are examples of this method; so too are the Spanish and Portuguese colonizations of Mexico and of South America. The Achaean colonies of Greater Greece in Southern Italy furnish additional and very important instances of this development of territorial feudal States by sea nomads: "This Achaean League of cities was a true colonization. The cities were without harbors—Croton only had a fair roadstead—*and were without any trade of their own*; the Sybarite could boast of his growing gray in his water town between his home bridges, while buying and selling were carried on by Milesians and Etruscans. On the other hand, the Greeks in this region not only controlled the fringe of the shore, but ruled from sea to sea; . . . the native agricultural inhabitants were forced into a relation of clientage or serfdom, and were required to work the farms of their masters or to pay tribute to them."[80] It is probable that most of the Doric colonies in Crete were similarly organized.

But in the course of universal history these "territorial States," whether they arose more or less frequently, did not acquire any such importance as did those maritime cities which devoted their principal energies to commerce and to privateering. Mommsen contrasts in distinct and well chosen sentences the Achaean landed squire with the "royal merchants" of the Greek Colonies in Southern Italy: "In no way did they spurn agriculture or the increase of territory; the Greeks were not satisfied, at least not after they became powerful, to remain within the confined space of a fortified commercial factory in the midst of the country of the barbarians, as the Phoenicians had done. Their cities were founded primarily and exclusively for purposes of trade, and unlike the

Achaean colonies, were universally situated at the best harbors and landing places."[81] We are certain, in the case of the Ionic colonies, and may well assume it for the other cases, that the founders of these cities were not landed squires, but seafaring merchants.

But such maritime States or cities, in the strict sense, came into being not only through warlike conquest, but also through peaceable beginnings, by a more or less mixed *pénétration pacifique*.

Where, however, the Vikings did not meet peaceable peasants, but feudal States in the primitive stage, willing to fight, they offered and accepted terms of peace and settled down as colonies of merchants.

We know of such cases from every part of the world, in harbors and on markets held on shore. To take the instances with which Germans are most conversant, there are the settlements of North German merchants in countries along the German ocean and the Baltic Sea, the German Steel Yard in London, the Hansa in Sweden and Norway, on the Island of Schönen, and in Russia, at Novgorod. In Wilna, the capital of the Grand Dukes of Lithuania, there was such a colony; and the Fondaco dei Tedeschi in Venice is another example of a similar institution. The strangers in nearly every instance settle down as a compact mass, subject to their own laws and their own jurisdiction. They often acquire great political influence, sometimes extending to dominion over the State. One would think the following tale of Ratzel, concerning the coast and islands of the Indian Ocean, were a contemporaneous narrative of the Phoenician or Greek invasion of the Mediterranean at about 1,000 B.C.: "Whole nations have, so to say, been liquefied by trade, especially the proverbially clever, zealous, omnipresent Malays of Sumatra; as well as the treacherous Bugi of Celebes. These can be met with at every place from Singapore to New Guinea. Latterly, especially in Borneo, they have immigrated in masses on the call of the Borneo chieftains. Their influence was so strong that they were permitted *to govern themselves according to their own laws*, and they felt themselves so strong *that repeatedly they attempted to achieve independence*. The Achinese formerly occupied a similar position. Malacca had been made the principal mart by Malays from Sumatra, and after its decline, Achin became the most frequented harbor of this distant east, especially for the first quarter of the seventeenth century, the pivotal period of the development of that corner of the world."[82] The following, from among numberless instances, demonstrate the universality of this form of settlement: "In Urga, *where they politically dominate*, the merchants are crowded together into a separate Chinese Town."[83] In the Jewish States there were "small colonies of foreign merchants and mechanics, set apart in distinct quarters of the cities. Here, under the king's protection, they could live according to their own religious customs."[84] We may also compare with this, First Kings XX, 34. "King Omri of Ephraim was forced by the military success of his opponent, the King of Damascus, to grant to the Aramaic merchants the use of certain parts of the city of Samaria, where under royal protection they could trade. Later, when the turn of war favored his successor, Ahab, the latter demanded the same privilege for the Ephraimitic merchants in Damascus."[85] "The inhabitants of Italy, wherever they were, held together as solid and organized masses, the soldiers as legionaires, the merchants of all large cities as corporations; while the Roman citizens domiciled or dwelling in the various provincial *circuits*, were organized as a 'convention of Roman citizens' with their own communal government."[86] We may recall the mediaeval Ghettos, which, before the great persecution of the Jews in the Middle Ages, were similar merchant colonies. The settlements of Europeans in the ports of strong foreign empires at the present time show similar corporate organizations, having their own constitution and (consular) jurisdiction. China, Turkey and Morocco must continue to bear this mark of inferiority, while recently Japan has been able to rid herself of that badge.

The most interesting point about these colonies, at least for our study, consists in their general tendency to extend their political influence into complete domination. And there is good reason for this. Merchants have a mass of movable wealth, which is likely to be used as a decisive factor in the political upheavals constantly disturbing all feudal States, be it in international wars between two neighboring States, or in intra-national fights, such as wars of succession. In addition to this the colonists, in many cases, may rely on the power of their home State, basing their claim on ties of blood and on uncommonly strong commercial interests, while there is besides, the fact that in many cases they have in their warlike sailor-folk and their numerous slaves an effective and compact force of their own, capable of accomplishing much in a limited sphere.

The following story of the role played by Arab merchants in East Africa appears to me to show a historical type heretofore not sufficiently appreciated: "When Speke, as the first European, made this trip in 1857, the Arabs were merchants, living as aliens in the land. When in 1861 he passed the same way, the Arabs resembled great landed proprietors with rich estates and were waging war with the native territorial ruler. This process, repeatedly found in many other regions in the interior of Africa, is the necessary consequence of the balance of power. The foreign merchants, be they Arabs or Suaheli, ask the privilege of transit and pay tribute for it; they establish warehouses, which the chiefs favor, as these seem both to satisfy their vanity and to extend their connections; then incurring the suspicion, oppression and persecution of the chiefs, the merchants refuse to pay the rack tolls and dues, which have grown with their increased prosperity. At last, in one of the inevitable fights for the succession, the Arabs take the side of one pretender if he is pliable enough, and are thus brought into internal quarrels of the country and take part in the often endless wars."[87]

This political activity of the merchant denizens (*metoikoi*) is a constantly recurring type. "In Borneo there developed from the settlements of Chinese gold diggers separate States."[88] Properly speaking, the entire history of colonization by Europeans is a series of examples of the law that, with any superior force, the factories and larger settlements of foreigners tend to grow into domination, unless they approximate to the primal type of simple piracy, such as the Spanish and Portuguese conquests, or the East India Companies, both the English and the Dutch. "There lies a robber State beside the ocean, between the Rhine and the Scheldt," are the accusing words of the Dutch Multatuli. All East Asiatic, American and African colonies of all European peoples arose as one or the other of these two types.

But the aliens do not always obtain unconditional mastery. Sometimes the host State is too strong, and the newcomers remain politically powerless but protected aliens; as, for example, the Germans in England. Sometimes the host State, although subjugated, becomes strong enough to shake off the foreign domination; so, for instance, Sweden drove out the Hanseats who had imposed on her their sovereignty. In some cases, a conqueror overcomes both merchants and host State, and subjugates both; as happened to the republics of Novgorod and Pskov, when the Russians annexed them. In many cases, however, the rich foreigners and the domestic nobility amalgamate into one group of rulers, following the type of the formation of territorial States, in which we saw this take place whenever two about equally strong groups of rulers came into conflict. It seems to me that this last named situation is the most probable assumption for the genesis of the most important city States of antiquity, for the Greek maritime cities, and for Rome.

Of Greek history, to use the terms of Kurt Breysig, we know only the "Middle Ages," of Roman history, only its "Modern Times." For the matters that preceded, we must be extremely careful in drawing deductions from fancied analogies. But it seems to me that enough facts are proved and admitted to permit the conclusion that Athens, Corinth, Mycenae, Rome, etc., became States in the manner already set forth. And this would follow, even if the data from all known demography and general history were not of such universal validity as to permit the conclusion itself.

We know accurately from the names of places (Salamis: Island of Peace, equivalent to Market-Island), from the names of heroes, from monuments, and from immediate tradition, that in many Greek harbors there existed Phoenician factories, while the *hinterland* was occupied by small feudal States with the typical articulation of nobles, common freemen, and slaves. It can not seriously be disputed that the development of the city States was powerfully advanced by foreign influences; and this is true, though no specific evidence can be adduced to show that any of the Phoenician, or of the still more powerful Carian merchants were either allowed to intermarry with the families of the resident nobility, or were made full citizens, or finally even became princes.

The same applies to Rome, concerning which Mommsen, a cautious author, states: "Rome owes its importance, if not its origin, to these commercial and strategic relations. Evidence of this is found in many traces of far greater value than the tales of historical novels pretending to be authentic. Take an instance of the primaeval relations existing between Rome and Caere, which was for Etruria what Rome was for Latium, and thereafter was its nearest neighbor and commercial friend; or the uncommon importance attributed to the bridge over Tiber and the bridge building (Pontifex Maximus) in every part of the Roman State; or the galley in the municipal coat of arms. To this source may be traced the primitive Roman harbor dues to which, from early times, only those goods were subject which were intended for sale (*promercale*) and not what entered the harbor of Ostia, for the proper use of the charterer (*usuarium*), and which constituted therefore an impost on trade. For that reason we find the comparatively early use of minted money, and the commercial treaties of States oversea with Rome. In this sense, then, Rome may, as the story of its origin states, have been rather a created than a developed city, and among the Latin cities rather the youngest than the eldest."[89]

It would require the work of a lifetime of historical research to investigate these possibilities, or rather these probabilities; and then to write the constitutional history of these preeminently important city States, and to draw thence the very necessary conclusions. It seems to me that along this path there would be found much information on many an obscure question, such as the Etruscan dominion in Rome, or the origin of the rich families of Plebeians, or concerning the Athenian *metoikoi*, and many other problems.

Here we can only follow the thread which holds out the hope of leading us through the labyrinth of historical tradition to the issue.

ESSENCE AND ISSUE OF THE MARITIME STATES

All these are true "States" in the sociologic sense, whether they arose from the fortresses of sea-robbers, or from harbors of original land nomads as merchant colonies which obtained dominion or which amalgamated with the dominating group of the host people. For they are nothing but the organization of the political means, their form is domination, their content the economic exploitation of the subject by the master group.

So far as the principle is concerned, they are not to be differentiated from the States founded by land nomads; and yet they have taken a different form, both from internal and external reasons, and show a different psychology of classes.

One must not believe that class feeling was at all different in these and in the territorial States. Here as there the master class looks down with the same contempt on the subjects, on the "*Rantuses*," on the "man with the blue fingernails," as the German patrician in the Middle Ages looked on a being with whom, even when free born, no intermarriage or social intercourse was permitted. Little indeed does the class theory of the καλοικἀγαθοὶ (well-born) or of the patricians (children of ancestors) differ from that of the country squires. But other circumstances here bring about differences, consonant, naturally, with class interests. In any district ruled by merchants, highway robbery can not be tolerated, and therefore it is considered, e.g., among the maritime Greeks, a vulgar crime. The tale of Theseus would not in a territorial State have been pointed against the highwaymen. On the other hand, "piracy was regarded by them, in most remote times, as a trade nowise dishonorable . . . of which ample proof may be found in the Homeric poems; while at a much later period Polycrates had organized a well developed robber-State on the Island of Samos." "In the *Corpus Juris*, mention is made of a law of Solon in which the association of pirates (ἐπὶ λείαν οἰχόμενοι) is recognized as a permissive company."[90]

But quite apart from such details, mentioned only because they serve to cast a clear light on the growth of the "ideologic superstructure,"[*] the basic conditions of existence of maritime States, utterly different from those of territorial States, called into being two exceedingly important phenomena, which are of universal historical importance, viz., the growth of a *democratic constitution*, whereby the gigantic contest between the sultanism of the Orient and the civic freedom of the West was to be fought out (according to Mommsen the true content of universal history); and in the second place the development of *capitalistic slave-work*, which in the end was to annihilate all these States.

Let us first consider the inner or socio-psychological causes of this contrast between the territorial and the maritime State.

States are maintained by the same principle from which they arise. Conquest of land and populations is the *ratio essendi* of a territorial State; and by the repeated conquest of lands and populations it must grow, until its natural growth is checked by mountain ranges, desert, or ocean, or its sociological bounds are determined by contact with other States of its own kind, which it can not subjugate. The maritime State, on the other hand, came into being from piracy and trade; and through these two means, it must strive to extend its power. For this purpose, no extended territory need be absolutely subjected to its sway. There is no need to carry its development beyond the first five stages. The maritime States rarely, and only when compelled, proceed beyond the fifth stage, and attain to complete intra-nationality and amalgamation. Usually, it is

---

[*] How characteristic of these relations it is that Great Britain, the only "maritime State" of Europe, even at this present day will not surrender the right to arm privateers.

enough if other sea nomads and traders are kept away, if the monopoly of robbery and trade is secured, and if the "subjects" are kept quiet by forts and garrisons. Important places of production are, of course, actually "dominated"; and this applies especially to mines, to a few fertile grain belts, to woods with good lumber, to salt works, and to important fisheries. Domination here, therefore, means permanent administration, by making the subjects work these for the ruling class. It is only later in the development, that there arises a taste for "lands and serfs" and large domains for the ruling class *beyond the confines of the narrow and original limits of the State.* This happens when the maritime State by the incorporation of subjugated territories has become a mixture of the territorial and the maritime forms. But even in that case, and in contradistinction to territorial States, large landed properties are merely a source of money rental, and are in nearly all cases administered as absentee-property. This we find in Carthage and in the later Roman Empire.

The interests of the master class, which in the maritime State as well as in every other State, governs according to its own advantage, are different from those in the territorial State. In the latter the feudal territorial magnate is powerful because of his ownership of lands and people; while conversely, the patrician of the maritime city is powerful because of his wealth. The territorial magnate can dominate his "State" only by the number of men-at-arms maintained by him, and in order to have as many of these as possible, he must increase his territory as much as possible. The patrician, on the other hand, can control his "State" only by movable wealth, with which he can hire strong arms or bribe weak souls; such wealth is won faster by piracy and by trade than by land wars and the possession of large estates in distant territories. Furthermore, in order thoroughly to use such property, he would be obliged to leave his city to settle down on it, and to become a regular squire; because in a period when money has not yet become general, where a profitable division of labor between town and country has not yet come about, the exploitation of large estates can only be carried on by actually consuming their products, and absentee ownership as a source of income is inconceivable. Thus far, however, we have not reached that portion of the development. We are still examining primitive conditions. No patrician of any city State would, at this time, think of leaving his lively rich home, in order to bury himself among barbarians, and thus with one move cut himself off in his State from any political role. All his economic, social and political interests impel him with one accord toward maritime ventures. Not landed property, but movable capital, is the sinew of his life.

These were the moving causes of the actions of the master class in the maritime cities; and even where geographical conditions permitted an extensive expansion beyond the adjoining *hinterland* of these cities, they turned the weight of effort toward sea-power rather than toward territorial growth. Even in the case of Carthage, its colossal territory was of far less importance to it than its maritime interests. Primarily it conquered Sicily and Corsica more in order to check the competition of the Greek and Etruscan traders than for the sake of owning these islands; it extended its territories toward the Lybians largely to insure the security of its other home possessions; and finally, when it conquered Spain, its ultimate reason was the need of owning the mines. The history of the *Hansa* shows many points of similarity to the above. The majority of these maritime cities, moreover, were not capable of subjugating a large district. Even had there been the will to conquer, there were extraneous, geographical conditions that hindered. All along the Mediterranean, with the exception of some few places, the coastal plain is extremely narrow, a small strip fenced off by high mountain ranges. That was one cause which prevented most of the States grouped about some trading harbor from growing to anything like the size we should naturally assume to be probable; while in the open country, ruled by herdsmen, and this very early, immense realms came into being. The second cause for the small beginnings of these States is found in this, that the *hinterland* whether in the hills or on the few plains of the Mediterranean was occupied by warlike tribes. These tribesmen, either hunters or warlike herdsmen, or else primitive feudal States of the same master race as the sea nomads, were not likely to be subjugated without a severe contest. Thus in Greece the interior was saved from the maritime States.

For these reasons the maritime State, even when most developed, always remains centralized, one is tempted to say centered, on its trading harbor; while the territorial State, strongly decentralized from the start, for a long time continues to develop as it expands a still more pronounced decentralization. Later we shall see how this is affected by the adoption of those forms of government and of economic achievement which first were perfected in the "city-State," and which thus obtained the strength to counteract the centrifugal forces, and to build up the central organization which is characteristic of our modern States. This is the first great contrast between the two forms of the State.

No less decisive is the second point of contrast, whereby the territorial State remains tied up to natural economies as opposed to money economies, toward which the maritime State quickly turns. This contrast grows also out of the basic conditions of their existence.

Wherever a State lives in natural economy, money is a superfluous luxury—so superfluous that an economy developed to the use of money retrogrades again into a system of payments in kind as soon as the community drops back into the primitive form. Thus after Charlemagne had issued good coins, the economic situation expelled them. Neustria—not to mention Austrasia—under the stress of the migration of the peoples reverted to payment in kind. Such a system can well do without money as a standard of values, since it is without any developed intercourse and traffic. The lord's tenants furnish as tribute those things that the lord and his followers consume immediately; while his ornaments, fine fabrics, damascened arms, or rare horses, salt, etc., are procured in exchange with wandering merchants for slaves, wax, furs and other products of a warlike economic system of exchange in kind.

In city life, at any advanced stage of development, it is impossible to exist without a common measure of values. The free mechanic in a city can not, except in rare cases, find some other craftsman in need of the special thing which he produces, prepared to consume it immediately. Then, too, in cities the inevitable retail trade in food products, where every one must purchase nearly everything required, makes the use of coined money quite inevitable. It is impossible to conduct trade in its more limited sense, not between merchant and customers, but between merchant and merchant, without having a common measure of value. Imagine the case of a trader entering a port with a cargo of slaves, wishing to take cloth as a return cargo, and finding a cloth merchant who at the time may not want slaves but iron, or cattle, or furs. To accomplish this exchange, at least a dozen intermediate trades would have to take place before the object could be achieved. That can be avoided only if there exists some one commodity desired by all. In the system of payment in kind of the territorial States this may be taken by cattle or horses, since they may be used by anyone at some time; but the ship owner can not load with cattle as a means of payment, and thus gold and silver become recognized as "money."

From centralization and from the use of money, which are the necessary properties of the maritime or the *city State*, as we shall hereafter call it, its fate follows of necessity.

The psychology of the townsman, and especially of the dweller in the maritime commercial city, is radically different from that of the countryman. His point of view is freer and more inclusive, even though it be more superficial; he is livelier, because more impressions strike him in a day than a peasant in a year. He becomes used to constant changes and news, and thus is always *novarum rerum cupidus*. He is more remote from nature and less dependent on it than is the peasant, and therefore he has less fear of "ghosts." One consequence of this is that an underling in a city State is less apt to regard the "taboo" regulations imposed on him by the first and second estates of rulers. And as he is compelled to live in compact masses with his fellow subjects, he early finds his strength in numbers, so that he becomes more unruly and seditious than the serf who lives in such isolation that he never becomes conscious of the mass to which he belongs and ever remains under the impression that his overlord with his followers would have the upper hand in every fight.

This in itself brings about an ever progressive dissolution of the rigid system of subordinated groups first created by the feudal State. In Greece the territorial States alone were able to keep their subjects for a long time in a state of subjection: Sparta its Helots, Thessaly its *Penestoe*. In all the city States, on the other hand, we early find an uprising of the proletariat against which the master class was unable to oppose an effective resistance.

The economic situation tends toward the same result as the conditions of settlement. Movable wealth had far less stability than landed property: the sea is tricky, and the fortunes of maritime war and piracy not less so. The rich man of to-day may lose all by a turn of Fortune's wheel; while the poorest man may, by the same swing, land on top. But in a commonwealth based entirely on possessions, loss of fortune brings with it loss of rank and of "class," just as the converse takes place. The rich Plebeian becomes the leader of the mass of the people in their constitutional fight for equal rights and places all his fortune at risk in that struggle. The position of the patricians becomes untenable; when coerced they have ever conceded the claims of the lower class. As soon as the first rich Plebeian has been taken into their ranks, the right of rule by birth, defended as a holy institution, has forever become impossible. Henceforth it follows that what is fair for one is fair for the other; and the aristocratic rule is followed first by the plutocratic, then by the democratic, finally by the ochlocratic regime, until either foreign conquest or the "tyranny" of some "Savior of the Sword" rescues the community from chaos.

This end affects not only the State, but in most cases its inhabitants so profoundly that one may speak of a literal *death of the peoples*, caused by the *capitalistic exploitation of slave labor*. This latter is a social institution inevitably bound to exist in every State founded on piracy and maritime ventures and thus coming to use money as a means of exchange. In the primitive stages of feudalism, whence it was derived, slavery was harmless, as is true in all economic systems based on exchange and use in kind, only to become an ulcerating cancer, utterly destructive of the entire life of the State as soon as it is exploited by the "capitalist" method, i.e., as soon as slave labor is applied, not to be used in a system of a feudal payment in kind, but to supply a market paying in money.

Numberless slaves are brought into the country by piracy, privateering, or by the commercial wars. The wealth of their owners permits them to work the ground more intensively, and the owners of realty within the confines of the city limits draw ever increasing revenues from their possessions, and become more and more greedy of land. The small freeholder in the country, overburdened by the taxes and military service of wars waged in the interests of this great merchant class, sinks into debt, becomes a slave for debt, or migrates into the city as a pauper. But even so there is no hope for him, since the removal of the peasants has damaged the craftsmen and small traders, for the peasants were wont to purchase in the city, while the great estates, constantly increasing by the removal of the peasantry, supply their own needs by their own slave products. The evil attacks other parts of the body politic. The remaining trades are gradually usurped by masters exploiting slave labor, which is cheaper than free labor. The middle class thus goes to pieces; and a pauper, good-for-nothing mob, a genuine "bob-tail proletariat" comes into being, which, by reason of the democratic constitution achieved in the interim, is the sovereign of the commonwealth. The full course, political as well as military, is then a mere question of time. It may take place without a foreign invasion; which, however, usually sets in, when by reason of the physical breakdown caused by the immense depopulation, by the consumption of the people in its literal sense, the final stage is attained. This is the end of all these States. Within the scope of this treatise we can not dilate on this phase.

Only one city State was able to maintain itself throughout the centuries, because it was the ultimate conqueror of all the others, and because it was enabled to counteract the consumption of population by the only method of sanitation possible; by extensive recreations of middle class populations, both in cities and in country districts, as well as by vast colonizations of peasants on lands taken from the vanquished.

The Roman Empire was that State. But even this gigantic organism finally succumbed to the consumption of population, caused by capital-istic slave exploitation. In the interval, however, it had created the first *imperium*, i.e., the first tensely centralized State on a large scale, and had overcome and amalgamated all territorial States of both the Mediterra-nean shores and its neighboring countries, and had thereby for all time set before the world the model of such an organized dominion. In addition to this it had developed the organization of cities and of the system of money economy to such an extent that they never were utterly destroyed, even in the turmoil of the barbarian migration. In conse-quence of this, the feudal territorial States that occupied the territory of the former Roman Empire either directly or indirectly received those new impulses which were to carry them beyond the condition of the normal primitive feudal State.

V: THE DEVELOPMENT OF THE FEUDAL STATE

THE GENESIS OF LANDED PROPERTY

We now return, as stated above, to that point where the primitive feudal State gave rise to the city-State as an offshoot, to follow the upward growth of the main branch. As the destiny of the city-State was determined by the agglomeration of that form of wealth about which the State swung in its orbit, so the fate of the territorial State is conditioned by that agglomeration of wealth which in turn controls its orbit, the *ownership of landed property*.

In the preceding, we followed the economic differentiation in the case of the shepherd tribes, and showed that even here the law of the agglomeration about existing nuclei of wealth begins to assert its efficacy, as soon as the political means comes into play, be it in the form of wars for booty or still more in the form of slavery. We saw that the tribe had differentiated nobles and common freemen, beneath whom slaves, being without any political rights, are subordinated as a third class. This differentiation of wealth is introduced into the primitive State, and sharpens very markedly the contrast of social rank. It becomes still more accentuated by settlement, whereby private ownership in lands is created. Doubtless there existed even at the time when the primitive feudal State came into being, great differences in the amount of lands possessed by individuals, especially if within the tribe of herdsmen the separation had been strongly marked between the prince-like owners of large herds and many slaves, and the poorer common freemen. These princes occupy more land than do the small freemen.

At first, this happens quite harmlessly, and without a trace of any consciousness of the fact that extended possession of land will become the means of a considerable increase of social power and of wealth. Of this, there is at this time no question, since at this stage the common freemen would have been powerful enough to prevent the formation of extended landed estates had they known that it would eventually do them harm. But no one could have foreseen this possibility. Lands, in the condition in which we are observing them, have no value. For that reason the object and the spoils of the contest were not the possession of *lands*, but of the *land and its peasants, the latter being bound to the soil* (*glebae adscripti* of our later law) as labor substrat and labor motors, from the conjunction of which there grows the object of the political means, viz., ground rent.

Every one is at liberty to take as much of *the uncultivated land* existing in masses as he needs and will or can cultivate. It is quite as unlikely that any one would care to measure off for another parts of an apparently limitless supply, as that any one would apportion the supply of atmospheric air.

The princes of the noble clans, probably from the start, pursuant to the usage of the tribe of herdsmen, receive more "lands and peasants" than do the common freemen. That is their right as princes, because of their position as patriarchs, war lords, and captains maintaining their warlike suites of half-free persons, of servants, of clients, or of refugees. This probably amounts to a considerable difference in the primitive amounts of land ownership. But this is not all. The princes need a larger surface of the *"land without peasants"* than do the common freemen, because they bring with them their servants and slaves. These have, however, no standing at law, and are incapable, according to the universal concepts of folk law, of acquiring title to landed property. Since, however, they must have land in order to live, their master takes it for them, so as to settle them thereon. In consequence of this, the richer the prince of the nomad tribe the more powerful the territorial magnate becomes.

But this means that wealth, and with it social rank, is consolidated more firmly and more durably than in the stage of herdsman ownership. For the greatest herds may be lost, but landed property is indestructible; and men bound to labor, bringing forth rentals, reproduce their kind even after the most terrible slaughter, even should they not be obtainable full grown in slave hunts.

About this fixed nucleus of wealth, property begins to agglomerate with increasing rapidity. Harmless as was the first occupation, men must soon recognize the fact that rental increases with the number of slaves one can settle on the unoccupied lands. Henceforth, the external policy of the feudal State is no longer directed toward the acquisition of land

and peasants, but rather of peasants without land, to be carried off home as serfs, and there to be colonized anew. When the entire State carries on the war or the robbing expedition, the nobles obtain the lion's share. Very often however, they go off on their own account, followed only by their suites, and then the common freeman, staying at home, receives no share in the loot. Thus the vicious circle constantly tends rapidly to enlarge with the increasing wealth of the lands owned by the nobles. The more slaves a noble has, the more rental he can obtain. With this, in turn, he can maintain a warlike following, composed of servants, of lazy freemen, and of refugees. With their help, he can, in turn, drive in so many more slaves, to increase his rentals.

This process takes place, even where some central power exists, which, pursuant to the general law of the people, has the right to dispose of uncultivated lands; while it is, in many cases, not only by sufferance, but often by the express sanction of that authority. As long as the feudal magnate remains the submissive vassal of the crown, it lies in the king's interest to make him as strong as possible. By this means his military suite, to be placed at the disposal of the crown in times of war, is correspondingly increased. We shall adduce only one illustration to show that the necessary consequence in universal history is not confined to the well-known effect in the feudal states of Western Europe, but follows from these premises even under totally different surroundings: "The principal service in Fiji consisted in war duty; and if the outcome was successful it meant new grants of lands, including therein the denizens, as slaves, and thus led to the assumption of new obligations."[91]

This accumulation of landed property in ever increasing quantity in the hands of the landed nobility brings the primitive feudal State of a higher State to the "finished feudal state" with a complete scale of feudal ranks.

Reference to a previous work by the author, based on a study of the sources, will show the same causal connection for German lands;[92] and in that publication it was pointed out that in all the instances noted a process takes place, identical in its principal lines of development. It is only on this line of reasoning that one can explain the fact, to take Japan as an example, that its feudal system developed into the precise details which are well known to the students of European history, although Japan is inhabited by a race fundamentally different from the Aryans; besides (a strong argument against giving too great weight to the materialistic view of history) the process of agriculture is on a totally different technical basis, since the Japanese are not cultivators with the plow, but with the hoe.

In this instance, as throughout this book, it is not the fortune of a single people that is investigated; it is rather the object of the author to narrate the typical development, the universal consequences, of the same basic traits of mankind wherever they are placed. Presupposing a knowledge of the two most magnificent examples of the expanded feudal State, Western Europe and Japan, we shall, in general, limit ourselves to cases less well known, and so far as possible give the preference to material taken from ethnography, rather than from history in its more restricted sense.

The process now to be narrated is a change, gradually consummated but fundamentally revolutionary, of the political and social articulation of the primitive feudal State: *the central authority loses its political power to the territorial nobility; the common freeman sinks from his status, while the "subject" mounts.*

THE CENTRAL POWER IN THE PRIMITIVE FEUDAL STATE

The patriarch of a tribe of herdsmen, though endowed with the authority which flows from his war-lordship and sacerdotal functions, generally has no despotic powers. The same may be said of the "king" of a small settled community, where, generally speaking, he would exercise very limited command. On the other hand, as soon as some military genius manages to fuse together numerous tribes of herdsmen into one powerful mass of warriors, despotic centralized power is the direct, inevitable consequence.[93] As soon as war exists, the truth of the Homeric

οὐκ ἀγαθὴ πολυκοιρανὴ, εἷς κοίρανος ἔστω

εἷς βασιλεύς,

is admitted by the most unruly tribes, and becomes a fact to be acted on. The free primitive huntsmen render to their elected chief unconditioned obedience, while on the war-path; the free Cossacks of the Ukraine, recognizing no authority in times of peace, submit to their

---

⋆ "The rule of the many is not a good thing, over the many there should be one king."

hetman's power of life and death in times of war. This obedience toward their war-lord is a trait common to every genuine warrior psychology.

The leaders of the great migrations of nomads are all powerful despots: Attila, Omar, Genghis Khan, Tamerlane, Mosilikatse, Ketchwayo. Similarly, we find that whenever a mighty territorial State has come into being as the result of the welding together of a number of primitive feudal States, there existed in the beginning a strong central authority. Examples of this may be seen in the case of Sargon Cyrus, Chlodowech, Charlemagne, Boleslaw the Red. Sometimes, especially as long as the main State has not yet reached its geographical or sociologic bounds, the centralized authority is maintained intact in the hands of a series of strong monarchs, which degenerates, in some instances, to the maddest despotism and insanity of some of the Caesars: especially do we find flagrant examples of this in Mesopotamia and in Africa. We shall merely touch on this phase: the more so, as it has little general effect on the final development of the forms of government. This point should, however, be stated, that the development of the form of government of a despotism depends in the main, on what the *sacerdotal* status of the rulers may be, in addition to their position as war-lords, and whether or not they hold the monopoly of trade as an additional regalian right.

The combination of Caesar and Pope tends in all cases to develop the extreme forms of despotism; while the partition of spiritual and temporal functions brings it about that their exponents mutually check and counterbalance one another. A characteristic example may be found in the conditions prevailing among the Malay States of the East Indian Archipelago, genuine "maritime States," whose genesis is an exact counterpart of that of the Greek maritime States. Generally speaking, the prince has just as little power among these, as, shall we say, the king at the opening of the history of the Attic States. The chieftains of the clans (in Sulu the Dato, in Achin the Pangolima), as in the case of Athens, have the real power. But where, "as in Tobah, religious motives endow the rulers with the position of a Pope in miniature, an entirely different phase is found. The Panglima then depend entirely on the Rajah, and are merely officials."[94] To refer to a well-known fact, when the aristocrats and chiefs of the clans in Athens and in Rome abolished the kingdom, they preserved at least the old *title*, and granted its use to a dignitary otherwise politically impotent, in order that the gods might have their offerings presented in the accustomed manner. For the same reason, in many cases, the descendant of the former tribal king is preserved as a dignitary, otherwise totally powerless, while the actual power of government has long since been transferred to some war chief; as in the later Merovingian Empire, the Carolingian Mayors of the palace (Major-domus) ruled alongside a "long locked king," *rex crinitus*, of the race of Merowech, so, in Japan, the Shogun ruled beside the Mikado, and in the Empire of the Incas, the commander of the Inca beside the Huillcauma, who had been gradually limited to his sacerdotal functions.[*95]

In addition to the office of supreme pontiff, the power of the head of the State is frequently increased enormously by the trading mo-nopoly, a function exercised by the primitive chieftains as a natural consequence of the peaceful barter of guest-gifts. Such a trade monopoly, for example, was exercised by King Solomon; and latterly by the Roman Emperor Friedrich II.[†96]

As a rule, the negro chieftains are "monopolists of trading";[97] as is the King of Sulu.[98] Among the Galla, wherever the supremacy of a head chief is acknowledged, he becomes "as a matter of course, the tradesman for his tribe; since none of his subjects is allowed to trade with strangers directly."[99] Among the Barotse and Mabunda, the king is "according to the strict interpretation of the law, the only trader of her country."[100]

Ratzel notes, in telling language, the importance of this factor: "In addition to his witchcraft, the chief increases his power by a *monopoly of trading*. Since the chief is the sole intermediary in trade, everything desired by his subjects passes through his hands, and he becomes the donor of all longed-for gifts, the fulfiller of the fondest wishes. In such a system, there lie certainly the possibilities of great power."[101] If, in conquered districts where the power of government is apt to be more tensely exercised, there is added the monopoly of trade, the royal power may become very great.

---

* In Egypt we find a similar state of affairs, beside the bigoted Amenhotep IV, the Majordomus of the palace Haremheb, who "managed to unite in his hands the highest military and administrative functions of the empire, until he exercised the powers of a regent of the State." Schneider, *Civilization and Thought of the Ancient Egyptians*. Leipzig, 1907, page 22.

† Cf. *Acta Imperii,* or *Huillard-Breholles, H. D. Fred. II.*—*Translator.*

It may be stated as a general rule, that even in the apparently most extreme cases of *despotism*, no monarchical *absolutism* exists. The ruler may, undeterred by fear of punishment, rage against his subject class; but he is checked in no small degree by his feudal followers. Ratzel, in speaking of the subject generally, remarks: "The so-called 'court assemblage' of African or of ancient American chiefs is probably always a council. . . . Although we meet with traces of absolutism with all peoples on a low scale, even where the form of government is republican, the cause of absolutism is not in the strength of either the State or of the chieftain, but in the moral weakness of the individual, who succumbs without any effective resistance to the powers wielded over him."[102] The kingdom of the Zulu is a limited despotism, in which very powerful ministers of state (Induna) share the power; with other Caffir tribes it is a council, sometimes dominating both people and chieftains.[103] In spite of this control "under Tshaka every sneezing or hawking in the presence of the tyrant, as well as every lack of tears at the death of some royal kinsman, was punished with death."[104] The same limitation applies to the West African kingdoms of Dahomy and Ashanti, notorious because of their frightful barbarities. "In spite of the waste of human life, in war, slave trade, and human sacrifices, there existed at no place absolute despotism. . . . Bowditch remarks on the similarity of the system prevailing in Ashanti, with its ranks and orders, with the old Persian system as described by Herodotus."[105]

One must be very careful, and this may again be insisted upon, not to confuse despotism with absolutism. Even in the feudal States of Western Europe, the rulers exercised, in many cases, power of life and death, free from the trammels of law; but nevertheless such a ruler was impotent as against his "magnates." So long as he does not interfere with the privileges of the classes, he need not restrain his cruelty, and he may even occasionally sacrifice one of the great men; but woe to him were he to dare to touch the economic privileges of his magnates. It is possible to study this very characteristic phase, completely free, from the standpoint of law, and yet closely hemmed in by political checks, in the great East African empires: "The government of Waganda and Wanyoro is, in theory, based on the rule of the king over the whole territory; but in reality this is only the semblance of government, since, as a matter of fact, the lands belong to the supreme chieftains of the empire. It was they who represented the popular opposition to foreign influences, in the time of Mtesa; and Muanga did not dare, for fear of them, to carry out any innovations. Although the kingship is limited in reality, yet in form it occupies an imposing position in unessentials. The ruler is absolute master over the lives and limbs of his subjects, the mass of the people, and feels himself restrained only in the narrowest circle of the chief courtiers."[106]

Precisely the same statement applies to the inhabitants of Oceania, to mention the last of the great societies that created States: "At no place does one find an entire absence of a representative mediation between prince and people. . . . The aristocratic principle corrects the patriarchal. Therefore, the extremes of *despotism* depend more on class and caste pressure than on the overpowering will of any individual."[107]

THE POLITICAL AND SOCIAL DISINTEGRATION OF THE PRIMITIVE FEUDAL STATE

Space forbids our detailing the innumerable shadings under which the patriarchal-aristocratic (in some cases plutocratic) mixture of forms of government in the primitive feudal State is shown in either an ethnographic, historical or juristic survey. This is likewise of the greatest importance for subsequent development.

It is indifferent how much power the ruler may have had at the beginning, an inevitable fate breaks down his power in a short while; and does this, one may say, the faster, the greater that power was, i.e., the larger the territory of the primitive feudal State of higher grade.

Taking into account the process already set forth, which, through the occupation and settlement of unused lands by means of newly acquired slaves, made for the increase of power of the separate nobles, a result came about which might prove uncomfortable for the central power. Mommsen in speaking of the Celts says: "When in a clan numbering about eighty thousand armed men, a single chieftain could appear at convocation with ten thousand followers, exclusive of his serfs and debtors, it becomes clear that such a noble was rather an independent prince than a mere citizen of his clan."[108] And the same may apply to the "Heiu" of the Somali, where a great landed proprietor maintained hundreds of families in dependence on his lands, "so that conditions in Somaliland tend to recall those existing in mediaeval Europe during feudal times."[109]

Although such a preponderance of isolated territorial magnates can come about in the feudal State of low development, it nevertheless reaches its culmination in the feudal State of higher grade, the great feudal State; this happens by reason of the increased power given to the landlords by the bestowal of *public official functions.*

The more the State expands, the more must official power be delegated by the central government to its representatives on the borders and marches, who are constantly threatened by wars and insurrectionary outbreaks. In order to preserve his bailiwick in safety for the State, such an official must be endowed with supreme military powers, joined with the functions of the highest administrative officials. Even should he not require a large number of civil employees, he still must have a permanent military force. And how is he to pay these men? With one possible exception, to be noted hereafter, there are no taxes which flow into the treasury of the central government and then are poured back again over the land, since these presuppose an economic development existing only where money is employed. But in communities having a system of payments in kind, such as these "territorial States" all are, there are no taxes payable in money. For that reason, the central government has no alternative but to turn over to the counts, or border wardens, or satraps, the income of its territorial jurisdiction. Such an official, then, receives the dues of the subjects, determines when and where forced labor is to be rendered, receives the deodands, fees and penalties payable in cattle; etc.; and in consideration of these must maintain the armed force, place definite numbers of armed men at the disposal of the central government, build and maintain highways and bridges, feed and stable the ruler and his following, or his "royal messengers," and finally, furnish a definite "Sergeantry" consisting of highly valuable goods, easily transported to the court, such as horses, cattle, slaves, precious metals, wines, etc.

In other words, he receives an immensely large fief for his services. If previously he was not, he now becomes the greatest man in his country, though before he probably was the most powerful landlord in his official district. He will hereafter do exactly what his equals in rank are doing, although they may not have his official position; that is to say, he will, only on a larger scale, continue to settle new lands with ever newly recruited serfs. By this he increases his military strength; and this must be wished for and aided by the central government. For it is the fate of these States, that they must fatten those very local powers that are to engulf them.

Conditions arise which enable the warden of the marches to impose the terms of his military assistance, especially in the inevitable feuds which arise over the right of succession to the central government. Thereby he obtains further valuable concessions, especially the formal acknowledgment of the heritability of his official fief, so that office and lands come to be held by an identical tenure. By this means, he gradually becomes almost independent of the central authority, and the complaint of the Russian peasant, "The sky is high up and the Tsar is far off," tends to become of universal application. Take this characteristic example from Africa: "The empire of Lunda is an absolute feudal State. The chieftains (Muata, Mona, Muene) are permitted independent action in all internal affairs, so long as it pleases the Muata Jamvo. Usually, the great chieftains, living afar, send their caravans with their tribute once a year to the Mussumba; but *those living at too great a distance, sometimes for long periods omit making any payments of their tribute*; while similar chiefs forward tribute many times a year."[110]

Nothing can show more plainly than this report, how, because of inadequate means of transportation, extent of distance becomes politically effective in these States loosely held together and in a state of payment in kind. One is tempted to say that the independence of the feudal masters grows in proportion to the square of their distance from the seat of the central authority. The crown must pay more and more for their services and must gradually confirm them in all the sovereign powers of the State, or else permit their usurpation of these powers after they have seized them one after the other. Such are heritability of fiefs, tolls on highways and commerce, (in a later stage the right of coinage), high and low justice, the right to exact for private gain the public duties of repair of ways and bridges (the old English *trinodis necessitas*) and the disposal of the military services of the freemen of the country.

By these means, the powerful frontier wardens gradually attain an ever greater, and finally a complete, *de facto* independence, even though the *formal* bond of feudal suzerainty may for a long time apparently keep together the newly developed principalities. The reader, of course, recalls instances of these typical transitions; all mediaeval history is one chain of them; not only the Merovingian and Carolingian Empires, not only Germany, but also France, Italy, Spain, Poland, Bohemia, Hungary, as well as Japan and China,[111] have passed through this process of decomposition, not only once, but repeatedly. And this is no less true of the feudal States of Mesopotamia: great empires follow each other, acquire power, burst asunder time after time, and again are re-united. In the case of Persia, we are expressly told: "Separate States and provinces, by a successful revolt, obtained freedom for a longer or shorter time, and the 'great king' at Susa did not always have the power to force them to return to their obedience; in other States, the satraps or warlike chieftains ruled arbitrarily, carrying on the government faithlessly and violently, either as independent rulers or tributary under-kings of the king of kings. The Persian world-empire went to its disintegration an agglomeration of States and lands, without any general law, without ordered administration, without uniform judicial system, without order and enforcement of law, and without possibility of help."[112]

A similar fate overtook its neighbor in the valley of the Nile: "Princes spring from the families of the usurpers, free landlords, who pay land-taxes to nobody but to the king, and rule over certain strips of land, or districts. These district princes govern a territory specifically set apart as pertaining to their official position, and separate from their family possessions.

"Later successful warlike operations, perhaps filling in the gap between the Ancient and the Middle (Egyptian) Empire, *together with the gathering in of captives of the wars, who could be utilized as labor motors*, brought a more stringent exploitation of the subjects, a definite determination of the tributes. During the Middle Empire, the power of the princes of the clans rose to an enormous height, they maintained great courts, imitating the splendor of the royal establishment."[113] "With the decline of the royal authority during a period of decay, the higher officials use their power for personal aims, in order to make their offices hereditary within their families."*[114]

---

* Maspero says, *New Light on Ancient Egypt*, pp. 218–19: "Until then, in fact, the high priest had been chosen and nominated by the king; from the time of Rameses III he was always chosen from the same family, and the son succeeded his father on the pontifical throne. From that time events marched quickly. The Theban mortmain was doubled with a veritable seigniorial fief, which its masters increased by marriages with the heirs of neighboring fiefs,

But the operation of this historical law is not restricted to the "historical" peoples. In speaking of the feudal States of India, Ratzel states: "Even beyond Radshistan, the nobles often enjoyed a great measure of independence, so that even in Haiderabad, after the Nizam had acquired the sole rule over the country, the Umara or Nabobs maintained troops of their own, independently of the army of the Nizam. These smaller feudatories did not comply with the increased demands of modern times as regards the administration of Indian States as often as did the greater princes."[115]

In Africa finally, great feudal States come and pass away, as do bubbles arising and bursting from the stream of eternally similar phenomena. The powerful Ashanti empire, within one and a half centuries, has shriveled to less than one-fifth of its territory;[116] and many of the empires that the Portuguese encountered have since disappeared without leaving a trace of their existence. And yet these were strong feudal powers: "Stately and cruel negro empires, such as Benin, Dahomey or Ashanti, resemble in many respects ancient Peru or Mexico, having in their vicinity politically disorganized tribes. The hereditary nobility of the Mfumus, sharply separated from the rest of the State, had mainly the administration of the districts, and together with the more transitory nobility of service, formed in Loango strong pillars of the ruler and his house."[117]

But whenever such a State, once powerful, has split into a number of territorial States either *de facto* or juristically independent, the former process begins anew. The great State gobbles up the smaller ones, until a new empire has arisen. "The greatest territorial magnates later become emperors," says Meitzen laconically of Germany.[118] But even this great demesne vanishes, split up by the need of equipping warlike vassals with fiefs. "The Kings soon found that they had donated away all their belongings; their great territorial possessions in the Delta had melted away," says Schneider (l. c. page 38) of the Pharaohs of the sixth dynasty. The same causes brought

---

by continual bequests from one branch of the family to the other, and by *the placing of cadets of each generation at the head of the clergy of certain secondary towns.* The official protocol of the offices filled by their wives shows that a century or a century and a half after Rameses III, almost the whole of the Thebaid, about a third of the Egyptian territory, was in the hands of the High Priest of Ammon and his family."—*Translator's Note (and italics).*

about like effects in the Frankish Empire among both Merovingians and Carolingians; and later in Germany in the case of the Saxon and Hohenstaufen Emperors.[119] Additional references are unnecessary, as every one is familiar with these instances.

In a subsequent part of this treatise, we shall examine into the causes that finally liberated the primitive feudal State from this witch's curse, this circling from agglomeration to disintegration without end. Our present task is to take up the *social* side of the process, as we have already taken up the historical phase of it. It changes the articulation of classes in the most decisive manner.

The common freemen, the lower strata of the dominating group, are struck with overpowering force. They sink into bondsmenship. Their decay must go along with that of the central power; since both, allied one might say, by nature, are menaced simultaneously by the expanding power of the great territorial lords. The crown controls the landed magnate so long as the levy of the common freemen of the district is a superior force to his guards, to his "following." But a fatal need, already set forth, impels the crown to deliver over the peasants to the landed lordling, and from the moment when the county levy has become weaker than his guards, the free peasants are lost. Where the sovereign powers of the State are delegated to the territorial magnate, i.e., where he has developed more or less into an independent lord of the region, the overthrow of the liberties of the peasants is carried out, at least in part, under the color of law, by forcing excessive military services which ruin the peasants, and which are required the more often as the dynastic interests of the territorial lord require new lands and new peasants, or by abusing the right to compulsory labor or by turning the administration of public justice into military oppression.

The common freemen, however, receive the final blow either by the formal delegation or by the usurpation of the most important powers of the crown, the disposition of unoccupied lands or "commons." Originally, this land belonged to all the "folk" in common; i.e., to the freemen for common use; but in accordance with an original custom, probably universal, the patriarch enjoys disposal of it. This right of disposition passes to the territorial magnate with the remaining royal privileges and thus he has obtained the power to strangle any few remaining freemen. He now declares all unoccupied lands his property, *and forbids their settlement by free peasants* while those only are permitted access who recognize his superior lordship; i.e., who have commended themselves to him, or are his serfs.

That is the last nail in the coffin of the common freemen. Heretofore their equality of possessions has been in some way guaranteed. Even if a peasant had twelve sons, his patrimony was not split up, because eleven of them broke new hides of lands in the commons of the community, or else in the general land not yet distributed to other villages. That is henceforth impossible, hides tend to divide where large families grow up, others are united when heir and heiress marry: henceforth there come into existence "laborers," recruited from the owners of half, a quarter, or even an eighth of a hide who help work a larger area. Thus the free peasantry splits into rich and poor; this begins to loosen the bond which hitherto had made the bundle of arrows unbreakable. When, therefore, some comrade is overwhelmed by the exactions of the lord and has become his liegeman, or if bond peasants are settled among the original owners, either to occupy some hide vacated by the extinction of the family or fallen into the hands of the lord because of the indebtedness of its occupant, then every social cohesion is loosened; and the peasantry, split apart by class and by economic contrasts, is handed over without power of resistance to the magnate.

On the other hand, the result is the same where the magnate has no usurped regalian powers of the State. In such cases, open force and shameless violation of rights accomplish the same ends. The ruler, far off and impotent, bound to rely on the good will and help of the violators of law and order, has neither the power nor the opportunity of interference.

There is hardly any need of adducing instances. The free peasantry of Germany were put through the process of expropriation and declassification at least three times. Once it happened in Celtic times.[120] The second overthrow of the free peasants of the old German Empire took place in the ninth and tenth centuries. The third tragedy of the same form began with the fifteenth century, in the countries formerly Slavic, which they had conquered and colonized.[121] The peasants fared worse in those lands, in the "republics of nobles," where there was no monarchical central authority, whose community of interests with their subjects tended to deprive oppression of its worse features. The Celts in the Gaul of Caesar's time are one of the earliest examples. Here "the great families exercised an economic, military and political preponderance. They monopolized the leases of the lucrative rights of the State.

They forced the common freemen, overwhelmed by the taxes which they had themselves imposed, to borrow of them, and then, first as their debtors, afterward legally as their serfs, to surrender their liberty. For their own advantage they developed the system of followers: i.e., the privilege of the nobility to have about them a mass of armed servants in their pay, called *ambacti*, with whose aid they formed a State within a State. Relying on these, their own men-at-arms, they defied the lawful authorities and the levies of the freemen, and thus were able to burst asunder the commonwealth. . . . The only protection to be found was in the relation of serfdom, where personal duty and interest required the lord to protect his clients and to avenge any wrong to his men. Since the State no longer had the power to protect the freemen, these in growing number became the vassals of some powerful noble."[122] We find these identical conditions fifteen hundred years later in Kurland, Livonia, in Swedish Pomerania, in Eastern Holstein, in Mecklenburg, and especially in Poland. In the German territories the petty nobles subjugated their peasantry, while in Poland their prey was the formerly free and noble Schlachziz. "Universal history is monotonous," says Ratzel. The same procedure overthrew the peasantry of ancient Egypt: "After a warlike *intermezzo*, there follows a period in the history of the Middle Empire, which brings about a deterioration of the position of the peasantry in Lower Egypt. The number of landlords decreases, while their territorial growth and power increases. The tribute of the peasants is hereafter determined by an exact assessment on their estates, and definitely fixed by a sort of Doomsday Book. Because of this pressure, many peasants soon enter the lord's court or the cities of the local rulers, and take employment there either as servants, mechanics, or even as overseers in the economic organization of these manors or courts. In common with any available captives, they contribute to the extension of the prince's estates, and to further the general expulsion of the peasantry from their holdings."[123]

The example of the Roman Empire shows, as nothing else can, how inevitable this process becomes. When we first meet Rome in history the conception of serfdom or bondage has already been forgotten. When the "modern period" of Rome opens, only slavery is known. And yet, within fifteen centuries, the free peasantry again sink into economic dependence, after Rome has become an overextended, unwieldy empire, whose border districts have more and more dissolved from the central control. The great landed proprietors, having been endowed with the lower justice and police administration on their own estates, have "reduced their servants, who may originally have been free proprietors of the '*ager privatus vectigalis*' to a state of servitude, and have thus developed a sort of actual *glebae adscriptus*, within the boundaries of their 'immunities.' "[124] The invading Germans found this feudal order worked out in Gaul and the other provinces. At this particular time, the immense difference formerly existing between slaves and free settlers (*coloni*) had been completely obliterated, first in their economic position, and then, naturally, in their constitutional rights.

Wherever the common freemen sink into political and economic dependence on the great territorial magnates, when, in other words, they become bound either to the court or to the lands, the social group formerly subject to them tend in a corresponding measure to improve their status. Both layers tend to meet half-way, to approximate their position, and finally to amalgamate. The observations just made concerning the free settlers and the agricultural slaves of the late Roman Empire hold true everywhere. Thus in Germany, freemen and serfs together formed, when fused, the economic and legally unital group of *Grundholde* or men bound to the soil.[125]

The elevation of the former "subjects," hereafter for the sake of brevity to be called "plebs," flows from the same source as the debasement of the freeman, and arises by the same necessity from the very foundations on which these States are themselves erected, viz., the agglomeration of the landed property in ever fewer hands.

The plebs are the natural opponents of the central government—since that is their conqueror and tax imposer; while they naturally oppose the common freemen, who despise them and oppress them politically, besides crowding them back economically. The great magnate also is the natural opponent of the central government—an impediment in his path toward complete independence, and he is at the same time also a natural enemy of the common freemen, who in turn not only support the central government; but also block with their possessions his path toward territorial dominion, while with their claims to equality of political rights they annoy his princely pride. Since the political and social interests of the territorial princes and of the plebs coincide, they must become allies; the prince can attain complete independence only if, in his fight for power against the crown and the common freemen, he controls reliable warriors and acquiescent taxpayers; the plebs can only then be freed from their pariah-like declassification, both economically and socially, if the hated and proud common freemen are brought down to their level.

This is the second time that we have noted the identity of interest between the princes and their subjects. The first time we found a weakly developed solidarity in our second stage of State formation. This causes the semi-sovereign prince to treat his dependent tenants as kindly as he ill-treats the free peasants of his territory; in consequence, they will fight the more willingly for him and contribute taxes, while the more readily will the oppressed freemen succumb to the pressure, especially as their share of political power in the State, coincident with the decline of the central power, has become only a meaningless phrase. In some cases, as in Germany toward the end of the tenth century, this was done with full consciousness of its effects[126]—some prince exercises a particularly "mild" rule, in order to draw the subjects of a neighboring potentate into his lands, and thus to increase his own strength in war and taxation, and to weaken his opponent's. The plebs come to possess, both legally and actually, constantly increasing rights, enlarged privileges of the law of ownership, perhaps self-government in common affairs, and their own administration of justice; thus they rise in the same degree as the common freemen sink, until the two classes meet and they are amalgamated into one body on approximately the same jural and economic plane. Half serfs, half subjects of a State, they represent a characteristic formation of the feudal State, which does not as yet recognize any clear distinction between public and private law; in its turn an immediate consequence of its own historical genesis, *the dominion in the form of a State for the sake of economic private rights.*

THE ETHNIC AMALGAMATION

The juristic and social amalgamation of the degraded freemen and the uplifted plebs henceforth inevitably tends toward ethnic interpenetration. While at first the subject peoples were not allowed either to intermarry or to have social intercourse with the freemen, now no such obstacles can be maintained; in any single village the social class is no longer determined by descent from the ruling race, but rather by wealth. And the case may frequently arise where the pure-blooded descendant of the warrior herdsman must earn his living as a field hand in the hire of the equally pure-blooded descendant of the former serfs. The social group of the subjects is now composed of a part of the former ethnic master group and a part of the former subject group.

We say form a part only, because the other part has by this time been amalgamated with the other part of the old ethnic master group into a unital social class. In other words, a part of the plebs has not only attained the position to which the mass of the common freemen have sunk, but has climbed far beyond it, in that it has been completely received into the dominating group, which in the meantime, has not only risen enormously, but has been as greatly diminished in numbers.

And that, too, is a universal process found in all history; because everywhere it follows with equally compelling force from the very premises of feudal dominion. The *primus inter pares*, whether the holder of the central power or some local potentate, taking the rank of a prince, requires more supple tools for his dominion than are to be found among his "peers." The latter represent a class whom he must put down if he wants to rise—and that is and must be the aim of every one, since in this stage aiming for power is identical with the aim of self-preservation. In this effort he is opposed by his obnoxious and stiff-necked cousins and by his petty nobles—and for this reason, we find at every court, from that of the sovereign king of a mighty feudal empire down to the lord of what is hardly more than a big estate, men of insignificant descent as confidential officials alongside representatives of the master group, who in many cases under the mask of officials of the prince, as a matter of fact, are "ephors," sharers of the power of the prince as the plenipotentiaries of their group. Let us but recall the Induna at the court of the Bantu kings. There is no wonder, then, that the prince rather places confidence in his own men than in these annoying and pretentious advisers, in men whose position is indissolubly bound up with his own, and who would be ruined by his fall.*

---

* One of the most notable instances may be found in the case of Markward of Annweiler, Marquis of Ancona and Duke of Ravenna, seneschal of Henry VI, who after the death of the Emperor Henry VI disputed the power of the Regent Constance acting for her son, Frederick II. (See Boehmer-Ficker, *Regesta Imperii*, V, vol. I, No. 511. v. ad. annum 1197.)—*Translator.*

Here too, historical references are nearly superfluous. Every one is familiar with the fact that at the courts of the western European feudal kingdoms, besides the relatives of the king and some noble vassals, there were also elements from the lower groups, occupying high positions, clerics and great warriors of the plebeian class. Among the immediate following of Charlemagne all the races and peoples of his empire were represented. Also in the tales of Theodoric the Goth in the Dietrich Saga of the *Niebelungen Lied*, this rise of brave sons of the subject races finds its reflection. In addition to these, there follow some less well-known instances.

In Egypt, as far back as the Old Empire, there is found alongside the royal officials of the feudal nobility, who are the descendants of the Shepherd conquerors, administering their districts as representatives of the crown, with plenary powers as deputies, "*a mass of court officials* trusted with determined functions of government." It "originated with the *servants* employed at the courts of the princes, *such as prisoners of war, refugees etc.*"[127] The fable of Joseph shows a state of affairs known at that time to be a usual occurrence, of the rise of a slave to the position of an all powerful minister of State. At the present day such a career is within the realm of possibility at any Oriental court, such as Persia, Turkey, or Morocco, etc. In the case of old Marshal Derflinger, in the time of Friedrich Wilhelm I, the Great Elector, at a much later date, we have an example from the transition of the developed feudal State to a more modern form of the State, which might be multiplied by the examples of innumerable other brave swordsmen.

Let us add a few instances from the peoples "disregarded by history." Ratzel tells of the realm of Bornu: "The freemen have not lost the consciousness of their free descent, in contrast with the slaves of the sheik; but the rulers place more confidence in their slaves than in their own kinsmen and free associates of their tribe. They can count on the devotion of the former. Not only positions at court, but the defense of the country was from ancient times preferably confided to slaves. The brothers of the prince, as well as the more ambitious or more efficient sons, are objects of suspicion; and while the most important places at court are in the hands of slaves, the princes are put at posts far from the seat of government. Their salaries are paid from the incomes of the offices and the taxes from the provinces."[128]

Among the Fulbe "society is divided into princes, chieftains, commons and slaves. The slaves of the king play a great role as soldiers and officials, and may hope for the highest offices in the State."[129]

This nobility of the court's creation may, in certain cases, be admitted to the great imperial offices, so that according to the method stated above, it may achieve the sovereignty over a territory. In the developed feudal State it represents the high nobility; and usually manages to preserve its rank, even when some more powerful neighbor has mediatized it by incorporating the State. The Frankish higher nobility certainly contains such elements from the original lower group;[130] and since from its blood the entire upper nobility of the European civilized States has been descended at least in direct line by marriage, we find an ethnic amalgamation, both in the present day group of subjects and in the highest order of the ruling class. And the same applies to Egypt: "With the sinking of the royal authority in the time of the decay, the higher officials abuse their power for personal ends, to make their offices hereditary in their families, and thereby to call into existence an official nobility not differentiated from the rest of the population."[131]

And finally, the same process, from the same causes, takes hold of the present middle class, the lower stratum of the master class, the officials and officers of the great feudatories. At first there still exists a social difference between, on the one hand, the free vassals, the subfeudatories of the great landlord, kinsmen, younger sons of other noble families, impoverished associates from the same district, in isolated cases freeborn sons of peasants, free refugees and professional ruffians of free descent; and on the other, if the term may be allowed, the subalterns of the guards of plebeian descent. But lack of freedom advances, while freedom sinks in social value; and here too the ruler places more reliance on his creatures than on his peers. Here also, sooner or later, the process of amalgamation becomes complete. In Germany, as late as 1085, the non-free nobility of the court ranks between "*servi et litones*" while a century afterward it is placed with the "*liberi et nobiles*."[132] In the course of the thirteenth century, it has been completely absorbed, along with the free vassals, into the nobility by chivalry. The two orders in the meantime tend to become equal economically; both have subinfeudations, fiefs on the obligation of service in warfare, and the service feuds of the bondsmen; while all the fiefs of the "ministerials" or sergeants have in the meantime become as heritable as are those of the free vassals, as much so as are the patrimonies of the few surviving smaller territorial lords belonging to the original nobility, who may still have escaped the grasp of the great territorial principalities.

In ways quite analogous to this the development went on in all other feudal States of Western Europe; while its exact counterpart is found in the extreme Orient on the edge of the Eurasian continent, in Japan. The daimio are the higher nobility; the samurai, the chivalry, the nobility of the sword.

THE DEVELOPED FEUDAL STATE

With this the feudal State has reached its pinnacle. It forms, politically and socially, a hierarchy of numerous strata; of which, in all cases, the lower is bound to render service to the next above it, and the superior is bound to render protection to the one below. The pyramid rests on the laboring population, of whom the major part are as yet peasants; the surplus of their labor, the ground rental, the entire "surplus value" of the economic means is used to support the upper strata of society. This ground rent from the majority of estates is turned over to the small holders of fiefs, except where these estates are still in the immediate possession of the prince or of the crown and have not as yet been granted as fiefs. The holders of them are bound in return to provide the stipulated military service, and also, in certain cases, to render labor of an economic value. The larger vassal is in turn bound to serve the great tenants of the crown; who in their turn are, at least at strict law, under similar obligation toward the bearer of the central power; while emperor, king, sultan, shah, or pharaoh in their turn, are regarded as the vassals of the tribal god. Thus there starts from the fields, whose peasantry support and nourish all, and mounts up to the "king of heaven" an artificially graded order of ranks, which constricts so absolutely all the life of the State, that according to custom and law neither a bit of land nor a man can be understood unless within its fold. Since all rights originally created for the common freemen have either been resumed by the State, or else have been distorted by the victorious princes of territories, it comes about that a person not in some feudal relation to some superior must in fact be "without the law," be without claim for protection or justice, i.e., be outside the scope of that power which alone affords justice. Therefore the rule, *nulle terre sans seigneur*, appearing to us at first blush as an ebullition of feudal arrogance, is as a matter of fact the codification of an existing new state of law, or at the very least the clearing away of some archaic remnants, no longer to be tolerated, of the completely discarded *primitive* feudal State.

Those philosophers of history who pretend to explain every historic development from the quality of "races," give as the center of their strategic position the alleged fact, that only the Germans, thanks to their superior "political capacity," have managed to raise the artistic edifice of the developed feudal State. Some of the vigor of this argument has departed, since the conviction began to dawn on them that in Japan, the Mongol race had accomplished this identical result. No one can tell what the negro races might have done, had not the irruption of stronger civilizations barred their way, and yet Uganda does not differ very greatly from the empires of the Carolingians or of Boleslaw the Red, except that men did not have in Uganda any "values of tradition" of mediaeval culture: and these values were not any merit of the Germanic races, but a gift wherewith fortune endowed them.

Shifting the discussion from the negro to the "Semites," we find the charge made that this race has absolutely no capacity for the formation of States. And yet we find, thousands of years ago, this same feudal system developed by Semites, if the founders of the Egyptian kingdom were Semites. One would think the following description of Thurdwald were taken from the period of the Hohenstaufen emperors: "Whoever entered the following of some powerful one, was thereafter protected by him as though he had been the head of the family. This relation . . . betokens a fiduciary relation similar to vassalage. This relation of protection in return for allegiance tends to become the basis of the organization of all Egyptian society. It is the basis of the relations of the feudal lord to his sergeants and peasants, as it is that of the Pharaoh to his officials. The cohesion of the individuals in groups subject to common protecting lords, is founded on this view, even up to the apex of the pyramid, to the king himself regarded as 'vicar of his ancestors,' as the vassal of the gods on earth. . . . Whosoever stands without this social grasp, a 'man without a master,' is without the pale of protection and therefore without the law."[133]

The hypothesis of the endowment of any particular race has not been used by us, and we have no need of it. As Herbert Spencer says, it is the stupidest of all imaginable attempts to construct a philosophy of history.

The first characteristic of the developed feudal State is the manifold gradation of ranks built up into the one pyramid of mutual dependence. Its second distinctive mark is the amalgamation of the ethnic groups, originally separated.

The consciousness formerly existent of difference of *races* has disappeared completely. There remains only the *difference of classes*.

Henceforth we shall deal only with social classes, and no longer with ethnic groups. The social contrast is the only ruling factor in the life of the State. Consistently with this the ethnic group consciousness changes to a class consciousness, the theories of the group, to the theories of the class. Yet they do not thereby change in the least their essence. The new dominating classes are just as full of their divine right as was the former master group, and it soon is seen that the new nobility of the sword manages to forget, quickly and thoroughly, its descent from the vanquished group; while the former freemen now declassed, or the former petty nobles sunk in the social scale, henceforth swear just as firmly by "natural law" as did formerly only the subjected tribes.

The developed feudal State is, in its essentials, exactly the same thing as it was when yet in the second stage of State formation. Its form is that of dominion, its reason for being, the political exploitation of the economic means, limited by public law, which compels the master class to give the correlative protection, and which guarantees to the lower class the right of being protected, to the extent that they are kept working and paying taxes, that they may fufil their duty to their masters. In its essentials government has not changed, it has only been disposed in more grades; and the same applies to the exploitation, or as the economic theory puts it, "the distribution" of wealth.

Just as formerly, so now, the internal policy of these States swings in that orbit prescribed by the parallelogram of the centrifugal thrust of the former group contests, now class wars, counteracted by the centripetal pull of the common interests. Just as formerly, so now, its foreign policy is determined by the striving of its master class for new lands and serfs, a thrust for extension caused at the same time by the still existing need of self-preservation. Although differentiated much more minutely, and integrated much more powerfully, the developed feudal State is in the end nothing more than the primitive State arrived at its maturity.

VI: THE DEVELOPMENT OF THE CONSTITUTIONAL STATE

If we understand the outcome of the feudal State, in the sense given above, as further organic development either forward or backward conditioned by the power of inner forces, but not as a physical termination brought about or conditioned by outside forces, then we may say that the outcome of the feudal State is determined essentially by the independent development of social institutions called into being by the economic means.

Such influences may come also from without, from foreign States which, thanks to a more advanced economic development, possess a more tensely centralized power, a better military organization, and a greater forward thrust. We have touched on some of these phases. The independent development of the Mediterranean feudal States was abruptly stopped by their collision with those maritime States which were on a much higher plane of economic growth and wealth, and more centralized, such as Carthage, and more especially Rome. The destruction of the Persian Empire by Alexander the Great may be instanced in this connection, since Macedonia had at that time appropriated the economic advances of the Hellenic maritime States. The best example within modern times is the foreign influence in the case of Japan, whose development was shortened in an almost incredible manner by the military and peaceful impulses of Western European civilization. In the space of barely one generation it covered the road from a fully matured feudal State to the completely developed modern constitutional State.

It seems to me that we have only to deal with an abbreviation of the process of development. As far as we can see—though henceforth historical evidence becomes meager, and there are scarcely any examples from ethnography—the rule may be stated that forces from within, even without strong foreign influences, lead the matured feudal State, with strict logical consistency, on the same path to the identical conclusion.

The creators of the economic means controlling this advance are the cities and their system of money economy, which gradually supersedes the system of natural economy, and thereby dislocates the axis about which the whole life of the State swings; in place of landed property, mobile capital gradually becomes preponderant.

THE EMANCIPATION OF THE PEASANTRY

All this follows as a natural consequence of the basic premise of the feudal State. The more the great private landlords become a landed nobility, the more in the same measure must the feudal system of natural economy break to pieces. The more great landed property rights become vested in and nurtured by the princes of territorial States, the more is the feudal system based on payments in kind bound to disintegrate; one may say that the two keep step in this development.

So long as the ownership of great estates is comparatively limited, the primitive principle of the bee-keeper, allowing his peasants barely enough for subsistence, can be carried out. When, however, these expand into territorial dimensions, and include, as is regularly the case, accretions of land which are the results of successful warfare, or by the relinquishment and subinfeudation through heritage or political marriages of smaller land owners, scattered widely about the country and far from the master's original domains, then the policy of the bee-keeper can no longer be carried out. Unless, therefore, the territorial magnate means to keep in his pay an immense mass of overseers, which would be both expensive and politically unwise, he would have to impose on his peasants some fixed tribute, partly rental and partly tax. The economic need of an administrative reform unites, therefore, with the political necessity, to elevate the "plebs," in the way which has already been discussed.

The more the territorial magnate ceases to be a private landlord, the more exclusively he tends to become a subject of public law, viz., prince of a territory, the more solidarity mentioned above, between prince and people grows. We saw that some few magnates even as far back as the period of transition from great landed estates to principalities, found it to their greatest interest to carry on a "mild" government. This accomplished the result, not only of educating their plebs to a more virile consciousness toward the State, but also had the effect of making it easy for the few remaining common freemen to give up their political rights in return for protection; while it was still more important, in that it deprived their neighbors and rivals of their precious human material. When the territorial prince has finally reached complete *de facto* independence, his self interest must prompt him steadfastly to persevere in the path thus begun. Should he, however, again invest his bailiffs or officers with lands and peasants, he will still have the most pressing political interest to see to it that his subjects are not delivered to them without restraint. In order to retain his control, the prince will limit the right of the "knights" to incomes from lands to definite payments in kind and limited forced labor, reserving to himself that required in the public interests, such as forced labor on highways or on bridges. We shall soon come to see that the circumstance that in all developed feudal States the peasants have at least two masters claiming service, is decisive for their later rise.

For all these reasons, the services to be required of peasants in a developed feudal State must in some fashion be limited. Henceforth, all surplus belongs to him free from the control of the landlord. With this change, the character of landed property has been utterly revolutionized. Heretofore the landlord, as of right, was entitled to the entire revenue saving only what was absolutely necessary to permit his peasants to subsist and continue their brood; while hereafter, the total product of his work, as of right, belongs to the peasant, saving only a fixed charge for his landlord as ground rent. The possession of vast landed estates has developed into (*manorial*) rights. *This completes the second important step taken by humanity toward its goal.* The first step was taken when man made the transition from the stage of bear to that of the bee-keeper, and thereby discovered slavery; this step abolishes slavery. Laboring humanity, heretofore only *an object* of the law, now for the first time becomes an entity capable of enjoying rights. The *labor motor*, without rights, belonging to its master, and without effective guarantees of life and limb, has now become the taxpaying subject of some prince. Henceforth the economic means, now for the first time assured of its success, develops its forces quite differently. The peasant works with incomparably more industry and care, obtains more than he needs, and thereby calls into being the "city" in the economic sense of the term, viz., the industrial city. The surplus produced by the peasantry calls into being a demand for objects not produced in the peasant economy; while at the same time, the more intensive agriculture brings about a reduction of those industrial by-products heretofore worked out by the peasant house industry.

Since agriculture and cattle-raising absorb in ever increasing degrees the energies of the rural family, it becomes possible and necessary to divide labor between original production and manufacture; the village tends to become primarily the place of the former, the industrial city comes into being as the seat of the latter.

THE GENESIS OF THE INDUSTRIAL STATE

L et there be no misunderstanding: we do not maintain that the city comes thus into being, but only the *industrial city*. There has been in existence the real historical city, to be found in every developed feudal State. Such cities came into being either because of a purely political means, as a stronghold,[134] or by the cooperation of the political with economic means, *as a market place*, or because of some religious need, as the environs of some temple.★ Wherever such a city in the historical sense exists in the neighborhood, the newly arising industrial city tends to grow up about it; otherwise it develops spontaneously from the existing and matured division of labor. As a rule, it will in its turn grow into a stronghold and have its own places of worship.

These are but accidental historical admixtures. In its strict economic sense "city" means the place of the economic means, or the exchange and interchange for equivalent values between rural production and manufacture. This corresponds to the common use of language, by which a stronghold however great, an agglomeration of temples, cloisters and places of pilgrimage however extensive, were they conceivable without any place for exchange, would be designated after their external characteristics as "like a city" or "resembling a city."

Although there may have been few changes in the exterior of the historical city, there has taken place an internal revolution on a magnificent scale. *The industrial city is directly opposed to the State.* As the State

---

★ "Every place of worship gathers about it dwellings of the priests, schools, and rest-houses for pilgrims."—Ratzel, l. c. II, p. 575.

   Naturally, every place toward which great pilgrimages proceed becomes an extended trade center. We may see the remembrances thereof in the fact that the great wholesale markets, held at stated times in Northern Europe, are called *Messen* from the religious ceremony.

is the developed political means, *so the industrial city is the developed economic means.* The great contest filling universal history, nay its very meaning, henceforth takes place between city and State.

The city as an economic, political body undermines the feudal system with political and economic arms. With the first the city *forces*, with the second it *lures*, their power away from the feudal master class.

This process takes place in the field of politics by the interference of the city, now a center of its own powers, in the political mechanism of the developed feudal State, between the central power and the local territorial magnates and their subjects. The cities are the strongholds and the dwelling places of warlike men, as well as depots of material for carrying on war (arms, etc.); and later they become central supply reservoirs for money used in the contests between the central government and the growing territorial princes, or between these in their internecine wars. Thus they are important strategic points or valuable allies; and may by far-sighted policy acquire important rights.

As a rule, the cities take the part of the crown in fights against the feudal nobles, from social reasons, because the landed nobles refuse to recognize the social equality, demanded as of right by their more wealthy citizens; from political reasons, because the central government, thanks to the solidarity between prince and people, is more apt to be influenced by common interests than is the territorial magnate, who serves only his private interests; and finally from economic reasons, because city life can prosper only in peace and safety. The practices of chivalry, such as club law, and private warfare, and the knights' practice of looting caravans are irreconcilable with the economic means; and therefore, the cities are faithful allies of the guardians of peace and justice, first to the emperor, later on, to the sovereign territorial prince; and when the armed citizenship breaks and pillages some robber baron's fortress, the tiny drop reflects the identical process happening in the ocean of history.

In order successfully to carry this political role the city must attract as many citizens as possible, an endeavor also forced on it by purely economic considerations, since both divisions of labor and wealth increase with increased citizenship. Therefore cities favor immigration with all their power; and once more show in this the polar contrast of their essential difference from the feudal landlords. The new citizens thus attracted into the cities are withdrawn from the feudal estates, which are thereby weakened in power of taxation and military defense in proportion as the cities are strengthened. The city becomes a mighty competitor at the auction, wherein the serf is knocked down to the highest bidder, to the one, that is to say, who offers the most rights. The city offers the peasant *complete liberty*, and in some cases house and courtyard. The principle, "city air frees the peasant" is successfully fought out; and the central government, pleased to strengthen the cities and to weaken the turbulent nobles, usually confirms by charter the newly acquired rights.

The third great move in the progress of universal history is to be seen in the discovery of the honor of free labor, or better in its rediscovery, it having been lost sight of since those far-off times in which the free huntsman and the subjugated primitive tiller enjoyed the results of their labor. As yet the peasant bears the mark of the pariah and his rights are little respected. But in the wall-girt, well-defended city, the citizen holds his head high. He is a freeman in every sense of the word, free even at law, since we find in the grants of rights to many early enfranchised cities (*Ville-franche*) the provision that a serf residing therein "a year and a day" undisturbed by his master's claim is to be deemed free.

Within the city walls there are still various ranks and grades of political status. At first the old settlers, the men of rank equal with the nobles of the surrounding country, the ancient freemen of the burgh, refuse to the newcomers, usually poor artisans or hucksters, the right of sharing in the government. But, as we saw in the case of the maritime cities, such gradations of rank can not be maintained within a business community. The majority, intelligent, skeptical, closely organized and compact, forces the concession of equal rights. The only difference is that the contest is longer in a developed feudal State, because now the fight concerns not only the parties at interest. The great territorial magnates of the neighborhood and the princes hinder the full development of the forces by their interference. In the maritime States of the ancient world, there was no *tertius gaudens* who could derive any profit from the contests within the city, since outside the cities there existed no system of powerful feudal lords.

These then, are the political arms of the cities in their contest with the feudal State: alliances with the crown, direct attack, and the enticing away of the serfs of the feudal lords into the enfranchising air of the city. Its economic weapons are no less effective: the change from payments in kind to the system of *money as a means of exchange* is inseparably connected with civic methods; it is the means whereby the method of payment in kind is utterly destroyed, and with it the feudal State.

THE INFLUENCES OF MONEY ECONOMY

The sociological process set into motion by the system of money economy is so well known and its mechanics are so generally recognized, that a few suggestions will suffice.

Here, as in the case of the maritime States, the consequence of the invading money system is that the *central government becomes almost omnipotent, while the local powers are reduced to complete impotence.*

Dominion is not an end in itself, but merely the means of the rulers to their essential object, the enjoyment without labor of articles of consumption as many and as valuable as possible. During the prevalence of the system of natural economy there is no other way of obtaining them save by dominion; the wardens of the marches and the territorial princes obtain their wealth by their political power. The more peasants who are owned, the greater is the military power and the larger the scope of the territory subjected, and thus the greater are the revenues. As soon, however, as the products of agriculture are exchangeable for enticing wares, it becomes more rational for every one to be primarily a private man, i.e., for every feudal lord not a territorial prince—and this now includes the knights—to decrease as far as possible the number of peasants, and to leave only such small numbers as can with the utmost labor turn out the greatest product from the land, and to leave these as little as possible. The net product of the real estate, thus tremendously increased, is now taken to the markets and sold for goods, and is no longer used to keep a fencible body of guards. Having dissolved this following, the knight becomes simply the manager of a knight's fee.★ With this event, as with one blow, the central power, that of king or territorial prince, is without a rival for the dominion, and has become politically omnipotent. The unruly vassals, who formerly made the weak kings tremble, after a short attempt at joint rule during the time of the government of the feudal estates, have changed into the supple courtiers, begging favors at the hands of some absolute monarch, like Louis XIV.

★ See reference as to the meaning of *Rittergutsbesitz*, ante, page 40.—*Translator.*

And he furthermore has become their last resort, since the military power, now solely exercised by him as the paymaster of the forces, alone can protect them from the ever-immanent revolt of their tenants, ground to the bone. While in the time of natural economy the crown was in nearly every instance allied with peasants and cities against nobility, we now have the union of the absolute kings, born from the feudal State, with their nobility, against the representatives of the economic means.

Since the days of Adam Smith it has been customary to state this fundamental revolution in some such form, as though the foolish nobles had sold their birthright for a mess of pottage, when they traded their dominion for foolish articles of luxury. No view can be more erroneous. Individuals often err in the safe-guarding of their interests; *a class for any prolonged period never is in error.*

The fact of the matter is, that the system of money payments strengthened the central power so mightily and immediately, that even without the interposition of the agrarian upheaval, any resistance of the landed nobility would have been senseless. As is shown in the history of antiquity, the army of a central government, financially strong, is always superior to feudal levies. Money permits the armament of peasant sons, and the drilling of them into professional soldiers, whose solid organization is always superior to the loose confederation of an armed mass of knights. Besides, at this stage, the central government could also count on the aid of the well-armed squires of the urban guilds.

Gunpowder did the rest in Western Europe. Firearms, however, are a product that can be turned out only in the industrial establishments of a wealthy city. Because of these technical military reasons, even that feudal landlord who might not care for the newly established luxuries and who might only be desirous of maintaining or increasing his independent position, must subject his territories to the same agrarian revolution; since in order to be strong, he now before all else must have *money*, which in the new order of things, has become the *nervus rerum*, either to buy arms or to engage mercenaries. A second capitalistic wholesale undertaking, therefore, has come into being through the system of payments in money; besides the wholesale management of landed estates, war is carried on as a great business enterprise—the condottieri appear on the stage. The market is full of material for armies of mercenaries, the discharged guards of the feudal lords and the young peasants whose lands have been taken up by the lords.

There are instances where some petty noble may mount to the throne of some territorial principality, as happened many a time in Italy, and as was accomplished by Albrecht Wallenstein, even as late as the period of the Thirty Years' War. But that is a matter of individual fate, not affecting the final result. The local powers disappear from the contest of political forces as independent centers of authority and retain the remnant of their former influence only so long as they serve the princes as a source of supplies; that is, the State composed of its feudal estates.

The infinite increase in the power of the crown is then enhanced by a second creation of the system of payment in money, by *officialdom*. We have told in detail of the vicious circle which forced the feudal State into a cul-de-sac between agglomeration and dissolution, as long as its bailiffs had to be paid with "lands and peasants" and thereby were nursed into potential rivals of their creator. With the advents of payments in money, the vicious circle is broken. Henceforth the central government carries on its functions through paid employees, permanently dependent on their paymaster.[135] Henceforth there is possible a permanently established, tensely centralized government, and empires come into being, such as had not existed since the developed maritime States of antiquity, which also were founded on the payments in money.

This revolution of the political mechanism was everywhere put into motion by the development of the money economy—with but one exception, as far as I can see, viz., Egypt.

Here, according to the statement of experts, no definite information is to be had, and it seems that the system of money exchanges appears as a matured institution only in Greek times. Until that time, the tribute of the peasants was paid in kind;[136] and yet we find, shortly after the expulsion of the Shepherd Kings, during the New Empire (*circa* sixteenth century B.C.), that the absolutism of the kings was fully developed: "The military power is upheld by foreign mercenaries, the administration is carried on by a *centralized body of officials* dependent on the royal favor, *while the feudal aristocracy has disappeared*."[137]

It may seem that this exception proves the rule. Egypt is a country of exceptional geographic conformation. Jammed into a narrow compass, between mountains and the desert, a natural highway, the River Nile, traverses its entire length, and permits the transportation of bulky freight

with much greater facility than the finest road. And this highway made
it easy for the Pharaoh to assemble the taxes of all his districts in his own
storehouses, the so-called "houses"[138] and from them to supply his
garrisons and civil employees with the products themselves *in natura*. For
that reason Egypt, after it has once become unified into an empire, stays
centralized, until foreign powers extinguish its life as a "State." "This
circumstance is the source of the enormous and plenary power exercised
by the Pharaoh where payments are still made in kind; the exclusive and
immediate control of the objects of daily consumption are in his hand.
The ruler distributes to his employees only such quantities of the entire
mass of goods as appears to him good and proper; and since the articles
of luxury are nearly all exclusively in his hands, he enjoys on this account
also an extraordinary plenitude of power."[139]

With this one exception, where a mighty force executes the task, the power
of circulating money seems in all cases to have dissolved the feudal State.

The cost of the revolution fell on peasants and cities. When peace is
made, the crown and the petty nobles mutually sacrifice the peasantry,
dividing them, so to say, into two ideal halves; the crown grants to the
nobility the major part of the peasants' common lands, and the greatest
part of their working powers that are not yet expropriated; the nobility
concedes to the crown the right of recruiting and of taxing both
peasantry and cities. The peasant, who had grown wealthy in freedom,
sinks back into poverty and therefore into social inferiority. The former
feudal powers now unite as allies to subjugate the cities, except where,
as in Upper Italy, these become feudal central powers themselves. (And
even in that case they for the most part fall into the power of captains
of mercenaries, condottieri.) The power of attack of the adversaries has
become stronger, the power of the cities has diminished. For with the
decay of the peasantry, their purchase power diminishes and with it the
prosperity of the cities, based thereon. The small cities in the country
stagnate and become poorer, and being now incapable of defense, fall a
prey to the absolutist rule of the territorial princes; the larger cities, where
the demand for the luxuries of the nobles has brought into being a strong
trading element, split up into social groups and thus fritter away their
political strength. The immigration now pouring into their walls is
composed of discharged and broken mercenaries, dispossessed peasants,
pauperized mechanics from the smaller towns; it is in other words a
proletarian immigration. For the first time there appears, in the terminol-

ogy of Karl Marx, the "free laborer," in masses, competing with his own class in the labor markets of the cities. And again, the "law of agglomeration" enters to form effective class and property distinctions, and thus to tear apart the civic population. Wild fights take place in the cities between the classes; through which the territorial prince, in nearly every instance, again succeeds in gaining control. The only cities that can permanently escape the deadly embrace of the prince's power are the few genuine "maritime States," or "city States."

As in the case of the maritime States, the pivot of the State's life has again shifted over to another place. Instead of circling about wealth vested in landed estates, it now turns about capitalized wealth, because in the meantime property in real estate has itself become "capital." *Why is it that the development does not, as in the case of the maritime States, open out into the capitalistic expropriation of slave labor?*

There are two controlling reasons, one internal, the other external. The external reason is to be found in this, that slave hunting on a profitable scale is scarcely possible at this time in any part of the world, since nearly all countries within reach are also organized as strong States. Wherever it is possible, as for instance, in the American colonies of the West European powers, it develops at once.

The internal reason may be found with the circumstances that the peasant of the interior countries, in contrast to the conditions prevailing in the maritime States, is subject, not to one master, but to at least two★ persons entitled to his service, his prince and his landlord. Both resist any attempt to diminish their peasants' capacity for service, since this is essential to their interests. Especially strong princes did much for their peasants, e.g., those of Brandenburg-Prussia. For this reason, the peasants, although exploited miserably, yet retained their personal liberty and their standing as subjects endowed with personal rights in all States where the feudal system had been fully developed when the system of payments in money replaced that of payments in kind.

★ In mediaeval Germany the peasants pay tribute in many cases not only to the landlord and to the territorial prince, but also to the provost and to the bailiff.

The evidence that this explanation is correct may be found in the relations of those States which were gripped by the system of exchange in money, before the feudal system had become worked out.

This applies especially to those districts of Germany formerly occupied by Slavs, but particularly to *Poland*. In these districts, the feudal system had not yet been worked out as thoroughly as in the regions where the demand for grain products in the great western industrial centers had changed the nobles, the subjects of public law, into the owners of a *Rittergut*,* the subjects of private economic interests. In these districts, the peasants were subject to the duty of rendering service only to *one* master, who was both their liege lord and landlord; and because of that, there came into being the republics of nobles mentioned above, which, as far as the pressure of their more progressed neighbors would permit, tended to approach the capitalistic system of exploiting of slave labor.[140]

The following is so well known that it can be Stated briefly. The system of exchange by means of money matures into Capitalism, and brings into being new classes in juxtaposition to the landowners; the capitalist demands equal rights with the formerly privileged orders, and finally obtains them by revolutionizing the lower plebs. In this attack on the sacredly established order of things, the capitalists unite with the lower classes, naturally under the banner of "natural law." But as soon as the victory has been achieved, the class based on movable wealth, the so-called middle class, turns its arms on the lower classes, makes peace with its former opponents, and invokes in its reactionary fight on the proletarians, its late allies, the theory of legitimacy, or makes use of an evil admixture of arguments based partly on legitimacy and partly on pseudo-liberalism.

In this manner the State has gradually matured from the primitive robber State, through the stages of the developed feudal State, through absolutism, to the modern constitutional State.

---

* See footnote on page 40.

THE MODERN CONSTITUTIONAL STATE

Let us give the mechanics and kinetics of the modern State a moment's time.

In principle, it is the same entity as the primitive robber State or the developed feudal State. There has been added, however, one new element—*officialdom*, which at least will have this object, that in the contest of the various classes, it will represent the common interests of the State as a whole. In how far this purpose is subserved we shall investigate in another place. Let us at this time study the State in respect to those characteristics which it has brought over from its youthful stages.

Its *form* still continues to be domination, its content still remains the exploitation of the economic means. The latter continues to be limited by public law, which on the one hand protects the traditional "distribution" of the total products of the nation; while on the other it attempts to maintain at their full efficiency the taxpayers and those bound to render service. The internal policy of the State continues to revolve in the path prescribed for it by the parallelogram of the centrifugal force of class contests and the centripetal impulse of the common interests of the State; and its foreign policy continues to be determined by the interests of the master class, now comprising besides the landed also the moneyed interests.

In principle, there are now, as before, only two classes to be distinguished: one a ruling class, which acquires more of the total product of the labor of the people—the economic means—than it has contributed, and a subject class, which obtains less of the resultant wealth than it has contributed. Each of these classes, in turn, depending on the degree of economic development, is divided into more or fewer subclasses or strata, which grade off according to the fortune or misfortune of their economic standards.

Among highly developed States there is found introduced between the two principal classes a transitional class, which also may be subdivided into various strata. Its members are bound to render service to the upper class while they are entitled to receive service from the classes below them. To illustrate with an example, we find in the ruling class in modern Germany at least three strata. First come the great landed magnates, who at the same time are the principal shareholders in the larger industrial undertakings and mining companies; next stand the

captains of industry and the "bankocrats," who also in many cases have
become owners of great estates. In consequence of this they quickly
amalgamate with the first layer. Such, for example, are the Princes
Fugger, who were formerly bankers of Augsburg, and the Counts of
Donnersmarck, owners of extensive mines in Silesia. And finally there
are the petty country nobles, whom we shall hereafter term *junker* or
"squires." The subject class, at all events, consists of petty peasants,
agricultural laborers, factory and mine hands, with small artisans and
subordinate officials. The "middle classes" are the classes of the transition:
composed of the owners of large and medium-sized farms, the small
manufacturers, and the best paid mechanics, besides those rich "bourgeois," such as Jews, who have not become rich enough to overcome
certain traditional difficulties which oppose their arrival at the stage of
intermarriage with the upper class. All these render unrequited service
to the upper class, and receive unrequited service from the lower classes.
This determines the result which occurs either to the stratum as a whole
or to the individuals in it; that is to say, either a complete acceptance
into the upper class, or an absolute sinking into the lower class. Of the
(German) transitional classes, the large farmers and the manufacturers of
average wealth have risen, while the majority of artisans have descended
to the lower classes. We have thus arrived at the kinetics of classes.

The interests of every class set in motion an actual body of associated
forces, which impel it with a definite momentum toward the attainment
of a definite goal. All classes whatever have the same goal; viz., the total
result of the productive labor of all the denizens of a given State. Every
class attempts to obtain as large a share as possible of the national
production; and since all strive for identically the same object, the *class
contest* results. This contest of classes is the content of all history of States,
except in so far as the interest of the State as a whole produces common
actions. These we may at this point disregard, since they have been given
undue prominence by the traditional method of historical study, and
lead to one-sided views. Historically this class contest is shown to be a
party fight. A party is originally and in its essence nothing save an
organized representation of a class. Wherever a class, by reason of social
differentiation, has split up into numerous sub-classes with varied
separate interests, the party claiming to represent it disintegrates at the
earliest opportunity into a mass of tiny parties, and these will either be
allies or mortal enemies according to the degree of divergence of the

class interests. Where on the other hand a former class contrast has disappeared by social differentiation, the two former parties amalgamate in a short time into a new party. As an example of the first case we may recall the splitting off of the artisans and Anti-Semite parties from the party of German Liberalism, as a consequence of the fact that the first represented descending groups, while the latter represented ascending ones. A characteristic example of the second category may be found in the political amalgamation which bound together into the farmers' union the petty landed squires of the East Elbian country with West Elbian rich peasants on large plantations. Since the petty squire sinks and the farmer rises, they meet half-way. All party policy can have but one meaning, viz., to procure for the class represented as great a share as is possible of the total national production. In other words, the preferred classes intend to maintain their share, at the very least, at the ancient scale, and if possible, to increase it toward such a maximum as shall permit the exploited classes just a bare existence, to keep them fit to do their work, just as in the bee-keeper stages. Their object is to confiscate the entire surplus product of the economic means, a surplus which increases enormously as population becomes more dense and division of labor more specialized. On the other hand, the group of exploited classes would like to reduce their tribute to the zero-point, and to consume the entire product themselves; and the transitional classes work as much as possible toward the reduction of their tribute to the upper classes, while at the same time they strive to increase their unrequited income from the classes underneath.

This is the aim and the content of all party contests. The ruling class conducts this fight with all those means which its acquired dominion has handed down to it. In consequence of this, the ruling class sees to it that legislation is framed in its interest and to serve its purpose—class legislation. These laws are then applied in such wise that the blunted back of the sword of justice is turned upward, while its sharpened edge is turned downward—class justice. The governing class in every State uses the administration of the State in the interest of those belonging to it under a twofold aspect. In the first place it reserves to its adherents all prominent places and all offices of influence and of profit, in the army, in the superior branches of government service, and in places on the bench; and secondly, by these very agencies, it directs the entire policy of the State, causes its class-politics to bring about commercial wars, colonial policies, protective tariffs, legislation in some degree improving the conditions of the laboring classes, electoral reform policies, etc. As long as the nobles ruled the State, they exploited it as they would have managed an estate; when the bourgeoisie obtain the mastery, the State is exploited as though it were a factory. And the class–religion covers all defects, as long as they can be endured, with its "don't touch the foundation of society."

There still exist in the public law a number of political privileges and economic strategic positions, which favor the master class: such as, in Prussia, a system of voting which gives the plutocrats an undue advantage over the less favored classes, a limitation of the constitutional rights of free assembly, regulations for servants, etc. For that reason, the *constitutional fight*, carried on over thousands of years and dominating the life of the State, is still uncompleted. The fight for improved conditions of life, another phase of the party and class struggle, usually takes place in the halls of legislative bodies, but often it is carried on by means of demonstrations in the streets, by general strikes, or by open outbreaks.

But the plebs have finally and definitely learned that these remnants of feudal strategic centers do not, except in belated instances, constitute the final stronghold of their opponents. It is not in political, but rather in economic conditions that the cause must be sought, which has brought it about that even in the modern constitutional State, the "distribution of wealth" has not been changed in principle. Just as in feudal times, the great mass of men live in bitter poverty; even under the best conditions, they have the meager necessities of life, earned by hard, crushing, stupefying forced labor, no longer exacted by right of political exploitation, but just as effectively forced from the laborers by their economic needs. And just as before in the unreformed days, the narrow minority, a new master class, a conglomerate of holders of ancient privileges and of newly rich, gathers in the tribute, now grown to immensity; and not only does not render any service therefore, but flaunts its wealth in the face of labor by riotous living. The class contest henceforth is devoted more and more to these economic causes, based on vicious systems of distribution; and it takes shape in a hand–to–hand fight between exploiters and proletariat, carried on by strikes, cooperative societies and trade unions. The economic organization first forces recognition, and then equal rights; then it leads and finally controls the political destinies of the labor party. In the end therefore the trade union controls the party. Thus far the development of the State has progressed in Great Britain and in the United States.

Were it not that there has been added to the modern State an entirely new element, its *officialdom*, the constitutional State, though more finely differentiated and more powerfully integrated, would, so far as form and content go, be little different from its prototypes.

As a matter of principle, the State officials, paid from the funds of the State, are removed from the economic fights of conflicting interests; and therefore it is rightly considered unbecoming for any one in the service of the government to be taking part in any money making undertaking, and in no well ordered bureaucracy is it tolerated. Were it possible ever thoroughly to realize the principle, and did not every official, even the best of them, bring with him that concept of the State held by the class from which he originated, one would find in officialdom, as a matter of fact, that moderating and order making force, removed from the conflict of class interests, whereby the State might be led toward its new goal. It would become the fulcrum of Archimedes whence the world of the State might be moved.

But the principle, we are sorry to say, can not be carried out completely; and furthermore, the officials do not cease being real men, do not become mere abstractions without class-consciousness. This may be quite apart from the fact that, in Europe at least, a participation in a definite form of undertakings—viz., handling large landed estates—is regarded as a favorable means of getting on in the service of the State, and will continue to be so as long as the landed nobility preponderates. In consequence of this, many officials on the Continent, and one may even say the most influential officials, are subject to pressure by enormous economic interests; and are unconsciously, and often against their will, brought into the class contests.

There are factors, such as extra allowances made by either fathers or fathers-in-law, or hereditary estates, and affinity to the persons in control of the landed and moneyed interest or allied with them, whereby the solidarity of interest among the ruling class is if anything increased from the fact that these officials, practically without exception, are taken from a class with whom since their boyhood days they have been on terms of intimacy. Were there, however, no such unity of economic interests the demeanor of the officials would be influenced entirely by the pure interests of the State.

For this reason, as a rule, the most efficient, most objective and most impartial set of officials is found in poor States. Prussia, for example, was formerly indebted to its poverty for that incomparable body of officials who handled it through all its troubles. These employees of the State were actually, in consonance with the rule laid down above, dissociated completely from all interests in money making, directly or indirectly.

This ideal body of officials is a rare occurrence in the more wealthy States. The plutocratic development draws the individual more and more into its vortex, robbing him of his objectivity and of his impartiality. And yet the officials continue to fulfil the duty which the modern State requires of them, to preserve the interests of the State as opposed to the interests of any class. And this interest is preserved by them, even though against their will, or at least without clear consciousness of the fact, in such manner that the economic means, which called the bureaucracy into being, is in the end advanced on its tedious path of victory, as against the political means. No one doubts that the officials carry on class politics, prescribed for them by the constellation of forces operating in the State; and to that extent, they certainly do represent the master class from which they sprang. But they do ameliorate the bitterness of the struggle, by opposing the extremists in either camp, and by advocating amendments to existing law, when the social development has become ripened for their enactment, without waiting until the contest over these has become acute. Where an efficient race of princes governs, whose momentary representative adopts the policy of King Frederick, which was to regard himself only as "the first servant of the State," what has been said above applies to him in an increased degree, all the more so as his interests, as the permanent beneficiary of the continued existence of the State, would before all else prompt him to strengthen the centripetal forces and to weaken the centrifugal powers. In the course of the preceding we have in many instances noted the natural solidarity between prince and people, as an historic force of great value. In the completed constitutional State, in which the monarch in but an infinitesimally small degree is a subject of private economic interests, he tends to be almost completely "an official." This community of interests is emphasized here much more strongly than in either the feudal State or the despotically governed State, where the dominion, at least for one-half its extent, is based on the private economic interests of the prince.

Even in a constitutional State, the outer form of government is not the decisive factor; the fight of the classes is carried on and leads to the same result in a republic as in a monarchy. In spite of this, it must be admitted that there is more probability, that, other things being equal, the curve of development of the State in a monarchy will be more sweeping, with less secondary incurvity, because the prince is less affected by momentary losses of popularity, is not so sensitive to momentary gusts of disapproval, as is a president elected for a short term of years, and he can therefore shape his policies for longer periods of time.

We must not fail to mention a special form of officialdom, the scientific staffs of the universities, whose influence on the upward development of the State must not be underestimated. Not only is this a creation of the economic means, as were the officials themselves, but it at the same time represents an historical force, the *need of causality*, which we found heretofore only as an ally of the conquering State. We saw that this need created superstition while the State was on a primitive stage; its bastard, the taboo, we found in all cases to be an effective means of control by the master class. From these same needs then, *science* was developed, attacking and destroying superstition, and thereby assisting in preparation of the path of evolution. That is the incalculable historical service of science and especially of the universities.

VII: The Tendency of the Development of the State

We have endeavored to discover the development of the State from its most remote past up to present times, following its course like an explorer, from its source down the streams to its effluence in the plains. Broad and powerfully its waves roll by, until it disappears into the mist of the horizon, into unexplored and, for the present-day observer, undiscoverable regions.

Just as broadly and powerfully the stream of history—and until the present day all history has been the history of States—rolls past our view, and the course thereof is covered by the blanketing fogs of the future. Shall we dare to set up hypotheses concerning the future course, until "with unrestrained joy he sinks into the arms of his waiting, expectant father"? (Goethe's *Prometheus*.) Is it possible to establish a scientifically founded prognosis in regard to the future development of the State?

I believe in this possibility. The tendency[141] of State development unmistakably leads to one point: seen in its essentials the State will cease to be the "developed political means" and will become "a freemen's citizenship." In other words, its outer shell will remain in essentials the form which was developed in the constitutional State, under which the administration will be carried on by an officialdom. But the content of the States heretofore known will have changed its vital element by the disappearance of the economic exploitation of one class by another. And since the State will, by this, come to be without either classes or class interests, the bureaucracy of the future will truly have attained that ideal of the impartial guardian of the common interests, which nowadays it laboriously attempts to reach. The "State" of the future will be "society" guided by self-government.

Libraries full of books have been written on the delimitation of the concepts "State" and "society." The problem, however, from our point of view has an easy solution. The "State" is the fully developed political

means, society the fully developed economic means. Heretofore State
and society were indissolubly intertwined: in the "freemen's citizenship," there will be no "State" but only "society."

This prognosis of the future development of the State contains by
inclusion all of those famous formulae, whereby the great philosophical
historians have endeavored to determine the "resulting value" of universal history. It contains the "progress from warlike activity to peaceful
labor" of Saint-Simon, as well as Hegel's "development from slavery to
freedom"; the "evolution of humanity" of Herder, as well as "the
penetration of reason through nature" of Schleiermacher.

Our times have lost the glad optimism of the classical and of the humanist
writers; sociologic pessimism rules the spirit of these latter days. The
prognosis here stated can not as yet claim to have many adherents. Not
only do the persons obtaining the profits of dominion, thanks to their
obsession by their class spirit, regard it as an incredible concept; those
belonging to the subjugated class as well regard it with the utmost
skepticism. It is true that the proletarian theory, as a matter of principle,
predicts identically the same result. But the adherents of that theory do not
believe it possible by the path of evolution but only through revolution. It
is then thought of as a picture of a "society" varying in all respects from that
evolved by the progress of history; in other words, as an organization of the
economic means, as a system of economics without competition and
market, as collectivism. The anarchistic theory makes form and content of
the "State" as inseparable as heads and tails of the coin; no "government"
without exploitation! It would therefore smash both the form and the
content of the State, and thus bring on a condition of anarchy, even if
thereby all the economic advantages of a division of labor should have to
be sacrificed. Even so great a thinker as the late Ludwig Gumplowicz, who
first laid the foundation on which the present theory of the State has been
developed, is a sociological pessimist; and from the same reasons as are the
anarchists, whom he combated so violently. He too regards as eternally
inseparable form and content, government and class-exploitation; since he
however, and I think correctly, does not consider it possible that many
people may live together without some coercive force vested in some
government, he declares the class State to be an "immanent" and not only
an historical category.

Only a small fraction of social liberals, or of liberal Socialists, believe
in the evolution of a society without class dominion and class exploita-

tion which shall guarantee to the individual, besides political, also economic liberty of movement, within of course the limitations of the economic means. That was the *credo* of the old social liberalism, of pre-Manchester days, enunciated by Quesnay and especially by Adam Smith, and again taken up in modern times by Henry George and Theodore Hertzka.

This prognosis may be substantiated in two ways, one through history and philosophy, the other by political economy, as a tendency of the development of the State, and as a tendency of the evolution of economics, both clearly tending toward *one* point.

The tendency of the *development of the State* was shown in the preceding as a steady and victorious combat of economic means against political means. We saw that, in the beginning, the right to the economic means, the right to equality and to peace, was restricted to the tiny circle of the horde bound together by ties of blood, an endowment from pre-human conditions of society;[142] while without the limits of this isle of peace raged the typhoon of the political means. But we saw expanding more and more the circles from which the laws of peace crowded out their adversary, and everywhere we saw their advance connected with the advance of the economic means, of the barter of groups for equivalents, amongst one another. The first exchange may have been the exchange of fire, then the barter of women, and finally the exchange of goods, the domain of peace constantly extending its borders. It protected the market places, then the streets leading to them, and finally it protected the merchants traveling on these streets.

In the course of this discussion it was shown how the "State" absorbed and developed these organizations making for peace, and how in consequence these drive back ever further right based on mere might. Merchants' law becomes city law; the industrial city, the developed economic means, undermines the feudal State, the developed political means; and finally the civic population, in open fight, annihilates the political remnants of the feudal State, and re-conquers for the entire population of the State freedom and right to equality; *urban* law becomes public law and finally international law.

Furthermore, on no horizon can be seen any force now capable of resisting effectively this heretofore efficient tendency. On the contrary, the interference of the past, which temporarily blocked the process, is obviously becoming weaker and weaker. The international relations of commerce and trade acquired among the nations a preponderating importance over the diminishing warlike and political relations; and in the intra-national sphere, by reason of the same process of economic development, movable capital, the creation of the right to peace, preponderates in ever increasing measure over landed property rights, the creation of the right of war. At the same time superstition more and more loses its influence. And therefore one is justified in concluding that the tendency so marked will work out to its logical end, excluding the political means and all its works, until the complete victory of the economic means is attained.

But it may be objected that in the modern constitutional State all the more prominent remnants of the antique law of war have already been chiseled out.

On the contrary, there survives a considerable remnant of these institutions, masked it is true in economic garb, and apparently no longer a legal privilege but only economic right, *the ownership of large estates—the first creation and the last stronghold of the political means.* Its mask has preserved it from undergoing the fate of all other feudal creations. And yet this last remnant of the right of war is doubtless the last unique obstacle in the pathway of humanity; and doubtless the *development of economics* is on its way to destroy it.

To substantiate these remarks I must refer the reader to other books, wherein I have given the detailed evidence of the above and can not in the space allotted here repeat it at large.[143] I can only re-state the principal points made in these books.

There is no difference in principle between the distribution of the total products of the economic means among the separate classes of a constitutional State, the so-called "capitalistic distribution," from that prevailing in the feudal State.

All the more important economic schools coincide in finding the cause in this, that the supply of "free" laborers (i.e., according to Karl Marx, politically free and economically without capital) perpetually exceeds the demand, and that hence there exists "the social relation of capital." There "are constantly two laborers running after one master for work, and lowering, for one another, the wages"; and therefore the "surplus value" remains with the Capitalist class, while the laborer never gets a chance to form capital for himself and to become an employer.

Whence comes this surplus supply of free laborers?

The explanation of the "bourgeois" theory, according to which this surplus supply is caused by the overproduction of children by proletarian parents is based on a logical fallacy, and is contradicted by all known facts.[144]

The explanation of the proletarian theory according to which the capitalistic process of production itself produces the "free laborers," by setting up again and again new labor-saving machines, is also based on a logical fallacy and is likewise contradicted by all known facts.[145]

The evidence of all facts shows rather, and the conclusion may be deduced without fear of contradiction, *that the oversupply of "free laborers" is descended from the right of holding landed property in large estates*; and that emigration into towns and oversea from these landed properties are the causes of the capitalistic distribution.

Doubtless there is a growing tendency in economic development whereby the ruin of vast landed estates will be accomplished. The system is their bleeding to death, without hope of salvation, caused by the freedom of the former serfs, the necessary consequence of the development of the cities. As soon as the peasants had obtained the right of moving about without their landlords' passport (German *Freizuegigkeit*), there developed the chance of escape from the countries which formerly oppressed them. The system of emigration created "the competition from oversea," together with the fall, on the Continent, of prices for farm products, and made necessary perpetually rising wages. By these two factors ground rent is reduced from two sides, and must gradually sink to the zero point, since here too no counterforce is to be recognized whereby the process might be diverted.[146] Thus the system of vast territorial estates falls apart. When, however, it has disappeared, there can be no oversupply of "free laborers." On the contrary "two masters will run after one laborer and must raise the price on themselves." There will be no "surplus value" for the Capitalist class, because the laborer himself can form capital and himself become an employer. By this the last remaining vestige of the political means will have been destroyed, and the economic means alone will exercise sway. The *content* of such a society is the "pure economics"[147] of the equivalent exchange of commodities against commodities, or of labor force against commodities, and the political *form* of this society will be the "freemen's citizenship."

This theoretical deduction is moreover confirmed by the *experience of history*. Wherever there existed a society in which vast estates did not exist to draw an increasing rental, there "pure economics" existed, and society approximated the form of the State to that of the "freemen's citizenship."

Such a community was found in the Germany of the four centuries[148] from about A.D. 1000, when the primitive system of vast estates was developed into the socially harmless dominion over vast territories, until about the year 1400, when the newly arisen great properties, created by the political means, the robber wars in the countries formerly Slavic, shut the settlers from the westward out of lands eastward of the Elbe.[149] Such a community was the Mormon State of Utah, which has not been greatly changed in this respect, where a wise land legislation permitted only small and moderate sized farm holdings.[150] Such a community was to be found in the city and county of Vineland, Iowa, U.S.A.,[151] as long as every settler could obtain land, without increment of rent. Such a commonwealth is, beyond all others, New Zealand, whose government favors with all its power the possession of small and middle-sized holdings of land, while at the same time it narrows and dissolves, by all means at its command the great landed properties, which by the way, owing to lack of surplus laborers, are almost incapable of producing rentals.[152]

In all these cases there is an astoundingly equalized well-being, not perhaps mechanically equal; but there is no wealth. *Because well-being is the control over articles of consumption, while wealth is the dominion over mankind.* In no such cases are the means of production, "capital," "producing any surplus values"; there are no "free laborers" and no Capitalism, and the political form of these communities approximates very closely to a "freemen's citizenship," and tends to approximate it more and more, so far as the pressure of the surrounding States, organized from and based on the laws of war, permits its development. The "State" decomposes, or else in new countries such as Utah or New Zealand, it returns to a rudimentary stage of development; while the free self-determination of free men, scarcely acquainted with a class fight, constantly tends to pierce through ever more thoroughly. Thus in the German Empire there was a parallel development between the political rise of the unions of the imperial free cities, the decline of the feudal States, the emancipation of the crafts, then still comprising the entire "plebs" of the cities, and the decay of the patrician control of the city government. This beneficent development was stopped by the erection of new primitive feudal States on the easterly border of the former German Empire, and thus the economic blossom of German culture was ruined. Whoever believes in a conscious purpose in history may say that the human race was again required to pass through another school of suffering before it could be redeemed. The Middle Ages had discovered the system of free labor, but had not developed it to its full capacity or efficiency. It was reserved for the new slavery of Capitalism to discover and develop the incomparably more efficient system of cooperating labor, the division of labor in the workshops, in order to crown man as the ruler of natural forces, as king of the planet. Slavery of antiquity and of modern Capitalism was once necessary; now it has become superfluous. According to the story, every free citizen of Athens disposed of five human slaves; but we have supplied our fellow citizens of modern society a vast mass of enslaved power, slaves of steel, that do not suffer in creating values. Since then we have ripened toward a civilization as much higher than the civilization of the time of Pericles, as the population, power, and riches of the modern communities exceeds those of the tiny State of Athens.

Athens was doomed to dissolution—by reason of slavery as an economic institution, by reason of the political means. Having once entered that pathway, there was no outlet except death to the population. Our path will lead to life.

The same conclusion is found by either the historical-philosophical view, which took into account the tendency of the *development of the State*, or the study of political economy, which regards the tendency of *economic development*; viz., that the economic means wins along the whole line; while the political means disappears from the life of society, in that one of its creations, which is most ancient and most tenacious of life, Capitalism, decays with large landed estates and ground rentals.

This has been the path of suffering and of salvation of humanity, its Golgotha and its resurrection into an eternal kingdom—from war to peace, from the hostile splitting up of the hordes to the peaceful unity of mankind, from brutality to humanity, from the exploiting State of robbery to the Freemen's Citizenship.

NOTES

1. "History is unable to demonstrate any one people, wherein the first traces of division of labor and of agriculture do not coincide with such agricultural exploitations, wherein the efforts of labor were not apportioned to one and the fruits of labor were not appropriated by some one else, wherein, in other words, the division of labor had not developed itself as the subjection of one set under the others."—Robertus-Jagetzow, *Illumination on the Social Question*, Second Edition. Berlin, 1890, p. 124. (Cf. *Immigration and Labor: The Economic Aspects of European Immigration to the United States*, by Dr. Isaac A. Hourwich. Putnam's, N.Y. 1912.—*Translator*.)

2. Achelis, *Die Ekstase in ihrer kulturellen Bedeutung*, vol. I of *Kulturprobleme der Gegenwart*, Berlin, 1902.

3. Grosse, *Formen der Familie*. Freiburg and Leipzig, 1896, p. 39.

4. Ratzel, *Völkerkunde*. Second Edition. Leipzig and Vienna, 1894–5, II, p. 372.

5. *Die Soziale Verfassung des Inkareichs*. Stuttgart, 1896, p. 51.

6. *Siedlung und Agrarwesen der Westgermanen, etc.* Berlin, 1895, I, p. 273.

7. l. c., I, p. 138.

8. Ratzel, l. c. I, p. 702.

9. Ratzel, l. c. II, p. 555.

10. Ratzel, l. c. II, p. 555.

11. For example with the Ovambo according to Ratzel, l. c. II, p. 214, who in part "seem to be found in slave-like status," and according to Laveleye among the ancient Irish (*Fuidhirs*).

12. Ratzel, l. c. I, p. 648.

13. Ratzel, l. c. II, p. 99.

14. Lippert, *Kulturgeschichte der Menschheit*. Stuttgart, 1886, II, p. 302.

15. Lippert, l. c. II, p. 522.

16. *Römische Geschichte*. Sixth Edition. Berlin, 1874, I, p. 17.

17. Ratzel, l. c. II, p. 518.

18. Ratzel, l. c. I, p. 425.

19. Ratzel, l c. II, p. 545.

20. Ratzel, l. c. II, pp. 390–1.

21. Ratzel, l. c. II, pp. 390–1.

22. Lippert, l. c. I, p. 471.

23. Kulischer, "The history of the development of interest from capital." *Jahrbücher für National Œkonomie.* III series, vol. 18, p. 318, Jena, 1899: (Says Strabo: "Plunderers and from the scant supplies of their native land covetous of the lands of others.")

24. Ratzel, l. c. I, p. 123.

25. Ratzel, l. c. I, p. 591.

26. Ratzel, l. c. II, p. 370.

27. Ratzel, l. c. II, pp. 390–1.

28. Ratzel, l. c. II, pp. 388–9.

29. Ratzel, l. c. II, pp. 103–4.

30. Thurnwald, *Staat und Wirtschaft im altem Ægypten. Zeitschrift für Soz. Wissenschaft,* vol. 4, 1901, pp. 700–1.

31. Ratzel, l. c. II, pp. 404–5. (Gumplowicz, *Rassenkampf,* p. 264. "Egypt, rich and self-sufficient, says Ranke, invited the avarice of neighboring tribes, who served other gods. Under the name of the Shepherd peoples, foreign dynasts and foreign tribes ruled Egypt for centuries.

  "Truly, the summary of universal history could not be begun with more characteristic words than those of Ranke. For in the words applied to Egypt the quintessence of the whole history of manknd is summed up."—*Translator.*)

32. Ratzel, l. c. II, p. 165.

33. Ratzel, l. c. II, p. 485.

34. Ratzel, l. c. II, p. 480.

35. Ratzel, l. c. II, p. 165.

36. Buhl, *Soziale Verhältnisse der Israeliten,* p. 13.

37. Ratzel, l. c. II, p. 455.

38. Ratzel, l. c. I, p. 628.

39. Ratzel, l. c. I, p. 625.

40. Cieza de Leon, "Seg. parte de la crónica del Peru." P. 75, cit. by Cunow, *Inkareich* (p. 62, note 1).

41. Cunow, l. c. p. 61.

42. Ratzel, l. c. II, p. 346.

43. Ratzel, l. c. II, pp. 36–7.

44. Ratzel, l. c. II, p. 221. (Cf. remarks by Hon. A. J. Sabath, M. C., *Sociological Argument on Workman's Compensation Bill*, p. 498, Senate Document 338, Sixty-second Congress, Second Session, Volume I. See also *Congressional Record* for March 1, 1913, Sixty-second Congress, Third Session, pp. 4503, 4529, *et seq.—Translator.*)

45. "Among the Wahuma, women occupy a higher position than among the negroes, and are watched carefully by their men. This makes mixed marriages difficult. The mass of the Waganda even to-day would not have remained a genuine negro tribe 'of dark chocolate colored skin and short wool hair' were it not that the two peoples are strictly opposed to one another as peasants and herdsmen, rulers and subjects, as despised and honored, in spite of the relations entered into among the upper classes. In the peculiar position, they represent a typical phenomenon, which is found repeated at many other points."—Ratzel, l. c. II, p. 177.

46. Ratzel, l. c. II, p. 178.

47. Ratzel, l. c. II, p. 198.

48. Ratzel, l. c. II, p. 476.

49. Ratzel, l. c. II, p. 453.

50. Kopp, *Griechische Staatsaltertümer*, 2, *Aufl.* Berlin, 1893, p. 23.

51. Uhland, *Alte hoch und niederdeutsche Volkslieder* I, 1844, p. 339, cited by Sombart: *Der moderne Kapitalismus*, Leipzig, 1902, I, pp. 384–5.

52. Inama-Sternegg, *Deutsche Wirtsch.-Gesch.* I, Leipzig, 1879, p. 59.

53. Westermarck, *History of Human Marriage*, London, 1891, p. 368.

54. Cf. Ratzel, l. c. I, p. 81.

55. Ratzel, l. c. I, p. 156.

56. Ratzel, l. c. I, pp. 259–60.

57. Ratzel, l. c. II, p. 434.

58. I. Kulischer, l. c., p. 317, where other examples may be found.

59. Westermarck, l. c., p. 400, which contains a number of ethnographical examples.

60. Westermarck, l. c., p. 546.

61. Cf. Ratzel, l. c. I, pp. 318, 540.

62. Ratzel, l. c. I, p. 106.

63. Ratzel, l. c. I, p. 335.

64. Ratzel, l. c. I, p. 346.

65. Ratzel, l. c. I, p. 347.

66. Buecher, *Entstehung der Volkswirtschaft*, Second Edition, Tübingen, 1898, p. 301.

67. Cf., Ratzel, l. c. I, p. 271, speaking of the islanders of the Pacific Ocean: "Intercourse from tribe to tribe is carried on by inviolable heralds, preferably old women. These act also as intermediary agents in trades." See also page 317 for the same practises among the Australians.

68. German Translation by L. Katscher. Leipzig, 1907.

69. Ratzel, l. c. I, p. 81.

70. Ratzel, l. c. I, pp. 478–9.

71. A. Vierkandt, *Die wirtschaftlichen Verhältnisse der Naturvölker. Zeitschrift für Sozialwissenschaft*, II, pp. 177–8.

72. Kulischer, l. c. pp. 320–1.

73. Lippert, l. c. I, p. 266, *et seq.*

74. Cf. Westermarck, l. c.

75. Ratzel, l. c. II, p. 27.

76. Herodotus IV, 23, cited by Lippert, l. c. I, p. 459.

77. Lippert, l. c. II, p. 170.

78. Mommsen, l. c. I, p. 139.

79. Similar conditions may be observed among the islanders near India. Here the Malays are vikings. "Colonization is an important factor, as conquest and settlement oversea . . . reminding one of the great role played in ancient Hellas by the roving tribes. . . . Every strip of coast line shows foreign elements, who enter uncalled for and in most instances spreading damage among the natives. The right of conquest was granted by the rulers of Tornate to noble dynasts, who later on became semi-sovereign viceroys on the islands of Buru, Serang, etc."

80. Mommsen, l. c. I, p. 132.

81. Mommsen, l. c. I, p. 134.

82. Ratzel, l. c. I, p. 160.

83. Ratzel, l. c. II, p. 558.

84. Buhl, l. c., p. 48.

85. Buhl, l. c., pp. 78–9.

86. Mommsen, l. c. II, p. 406.

87. Ratzel, l. c. II, p. 191; cf. also pp. 207–8.

88. Ratzel, l. c. I, p. 363.

89. Mommsen, l. c., p. 46.

90. Both cited by Kulischer, l. c., p. 319, from: Buechsenschuetz, *Besitz und Erwerb im griechischen Altertum*; and Goldschmidt, *History of the Law of Commerce*.

91. Ratzel, l. c. I, p. 263.

92. F. Oppenheimer, *Grossgrundeigentum und soziale Frage.* II, i. Berlin, 1898.

93. Nomadism is exceptionally characterized by the facility with which, from patriarchal conditions, despotic functions are developed with most far-reaching powers. Ratzel, l. c. Vol. II, pp. 388–9.

94. Ratzel, l. c. I, p. 408.

95. Cunow, l. c. pp. 66–7. Similarly among the inhabitants of the Malay Islands numerous examples are found in Radak (Ratzel, l. c. I, p. 267).

96. Buhl, l. c., p. 17.

97. Ratzel, l. c. II, p. 66.

98. Ratzel, l. c. II, p. 118.

99. Ratzel, l. c. II, p. 167.

100. Ratzel, l. c. II, p. 218.

101. Ratzel, l. c. I, p. 125.

102. Ratzel, l. c. I, p. 124.

103. Ratzel, l. c. I, p. 118.

104. Ratzel, l. c. I, p. 125.

105. Ratzel, l. c. I, p. 346.

106. Ratzel, l. c. II, p. 245.

107. Ratzel, l. c. I, pp. 267–8.

108. Mommsen, l. c. III, pp. 234–5.

109. Ratzel, l. c. II, p. 167.

110. Ratzel, l. c. II, p. 229.

111. Ratzel, l. c. I, p. 128.

112. Weber's, *Weltgeschichte,* III, p. 163.

113. Thurnwald, l. c., pp. 702–3.

114. Thurnwald, l. c., p. 712; cf. Schneider, *Kultur und Denken der alten Ægypter,* Leipzig, 1907, p. 38.

115. Ratzel, l. c. II, p. 599.

116. Ratzel, l. c. II, p. 362.

117. Ratzel, l. c. II, p. 344.

118. Meitzen, l. c. II, p. 633.

119. Inama-Sternegg, l. c. I, pp. 140–1.

120. Mommsen, l. c. V, p. 84.

121. Cf. the detailed exposition of this in Oppenheimer, l. c., II, iii.

122. Mommsen, l. c. III, pp. 234–5.

123. Thurnwald, l. c., p. 771.

124. Meitzen, l. c. I, pp. 362f.

125. Inama-Sternegg, l. c. I, pp. 373, 386.

126. Cf. Oppenheimer, l. c. p. 272.

127. Thurnwald, l. c., p. 706.

128. Ratzel, l. c. II, p. 503.

129. Ratzel, l. c. II, p. 518.

130. Meitzen, l. c. I, p. 579: "At the time of the compilation of the Lex Salica, the ancient racial nobility had been reduced to common freemen or else had been annihilated. The officials, on the other hand, are rated at threefold wergeld, 600 solidi, and if one be 'puer regis' 300 solidi."

131. Thurnwald, l. c., p. 712.

132. Inama-Sternegg, l. c. II, p. 61.

133. Thurnwald, l. c., p. 705.

134. "The larger camps of the army of the Rhine obtained their municipal annexes partly through army suttlers and camp followers, and particularly through the veterans, who after the completion of their services remained in their accustomed quarters. Thus there arose distinct from the military quarters proper a distinct town of cabins (Canabae). In all parts of the Empire, and especially in the various Germanias, there arose in the course of time, from these camps of the legionaries, and particularly from the headquarter stations, cities in the modern sense."—Mommsen, l. c. V, p. 153.

135. Eisenhardt, Gesch. der National Œkonomie, p. 9: "Aided by the new and more liquid means of payment in cash, it became possible to call into being a new and more independent establishment of soldiers and of officials. As they were paid only periodically it became impossible for them to make themselves independent (as the feudatories had done) and then to turn on their paymaster."

136. Thurnwald, l. c., p. 773.

137. Thurnwald, l. c., p. 699.

138. Thurnwald, l. c., p. 709.

139. Thurnwald, l. c., p. 711.

140. Cf. with this Oppenheimer, l. c. II, iii.

141. "Tendency, i.e., a law, whose absolute execution is checked by countervailing circumstances, or is by them retarded, or weakened." Marx, Kapital, vol. III, p. 215.

142. Cf. the excellent work of Peter Kropotkin, Mutual Aid in its Development.

143. Cf. F. Oppenheimer, *Die Siedlungsgenossenschaft etc.*, Berlin, 1896, and his *Grossgrundeigentum und soziale Frage.*

144. Cf. F. Oppenheimer, *Bevölkerungsgesetz des T. R. Malthus. Darstellung und Kritik*, Berlin-Bern, 1901.

145. Cf. F. Oppenheimer, *Grundgesetz der Marxschen Gesellschaftslehre, Darstellung und Kritik*, Berlin, 1903.

146. Cf. Oppenheimer, *Grundgesetz der Marxschen Gesellschaftslehre*, Part IV, particularly, the twelfth chapter: "Tendency of the Capitalistic Development."

147. Cf. Oppenheimer, *Grossgrundeigentum*, I, ii, Sec. 3, "Philosophy of the Social Body," pp. 57 *et seq.*

148. Cf. Oppenheimer, *Grossgrundeigentum*, II, ii, Sec. 3, p. 322.

149. Cf. Oppenheimer, *Grossgrundeigentum*, II, iii, Sec. 4, especially pp. 423 *et seq.*

150. Cf. F. Oppenheimer, "Die Utopie als Tatsache," *Zeitschrift für Sozial-Wissenschaft*, 1889, II, pp. 190 *et seq.*

151. Cf. Oppenheimer, *Siedlungsgenossenschaft*, pp. 477 *et seq.*

152. Cf. André Siegfried, *La démocratie en Nouvelle Zelande*, Paris, 1904.

INDEX

Index compiled by David Rosen.

Fox & Wilkes

Charles James Fox (1749–1806) inherited wealth and guidance from his father, who tutored him in gambling and who advised, "Never do today what you can put off 'till tomorrow." In 1768, just nineteen, the roguish Charles Fox took his seat in Parliament and quickly earned the esteem of his colleagues, Edmund Burke among them. The two joined forces on many causes, including that of the American Revolution, until Burke's horror over the French Revolution occasioned a permanent break. Fox fought for religious toleration, called for abolishing the slave trade, and advocated electoral reform. In defending his views he was a powerful orator, acknowledged as the ablest debater of his day. Neither party nor crown could dissuade him from following his own path. Above all things Fox hated oppression and intolerance, and in his passion for liberty transcended the conventional party politics of his day.

Like Fox, **John Wilkes** (1727–1797), too, could be extravagant in his passions. He married into his money and was an active member of the proudly blasphemous Hellfire Club. A few years after joining Parliament in 1757, he began a weekly journal, *The North Briton*, that became notorious for its wit and wickedness. In the famous issue #45 Wilkes assailed a speech given in the King's name; he was jailed for his temerity. His *Essay On Woman*, an obscene parody of Pope's *Essay On Man*, along with a reprinting of #45, led to further imprisonment and expulsion from Parliament. But the public rioted for his release and kept voting him back into office. Wilkes eventually won substantial damages and set important precedents regarding Parliamentary privilege and seizure of personal papers. After finally being allowed to rejoin Parliament in 1774 as Lord Mayor of London, he introduced libel legislation ensuring rights to jury trial, and continued to fight for religious tolerance and judicial and parliamentary reform. The monument on his grave aptly describes him as a friend of liberty.

Both Fox and Wilkes could be self-indulgent, even reckless in pursuit of their own liberty, but they never let personal foibles hinder them in championing the rights of the individual.